W9-BGU-384

FROM REAGAN—

"Reagan spelled backwards is nigger . . ."

TO RIOTING . . .

"The old Negro used to sit around whittling his stick and telling stories . . . He was beautiful; he was a philosopher and an orator . . . That old man in the ghetto is bitter now and he is the most dangerous Negro in the world."

"I don't believe in riots. In fact I turned in the cat who sold me my favorite suit . . ."

FROM WRITE-INS—

"To be forced to select between party dominated choices is to have no *real* choice at all . . . For a voter to write in a candidate of his own choosing represents the best instincts of the democratic process . . ."

TO ROLL-INS . . .

If I am elected President . . . "the traditional Easter Egg Roll on the White House lawn will be replaced by a Watermelon Roll . . . All White House dinner invitations will be handled by Eartha Kitt . . ."

THE MOST ENTERTAINING, PROVOCATIVE AND HONEST CAMPAIGN BOOK EVER WRITTEN!

WRITE ME IN!   DICK GREGORY

Books by Dick Gregory

Published by Bantam Books, Inc.

Write me in!
by Dick Gregory

EDITED BY JAMES R. MCGRAW

BANTAM BOOKS · TORONTO · NEW YORK · LONDON ®

WRITE ME IN!
A Bantam Book / published June 1968

PHOTOGRAPH CREDITS

*Courtesy of Sam Falk—*THE NEW YORK TIMES: *cover photograph;
The Day: photograph No. 17; Raymond Gaston: No. 3; Hud of
Greenwich Village: Nos. 4, 5; Stephen C. Rose: No. 2; Ted Rozu-
malski—*BLACK STAR: *Nos. 13, 14, 16, 19, 20; Flip Schulke—*BLACK
STAR: *No. 18*

*All rights reserved.
Copyright © 1968 by Dick Gregory.
This book may not be reproduced in whole or in part,
by mimeograph or any other means, without
permission. For information address:
Bantam Books, Inc.*

Published simultaneously in the United States and Canada

*Bantam Books are published by Bantam Books, Inc., a subsidiary
of Grosset & Dunlap, Inc. Its trade-mark, consisting of the words
"Bantam Books" and the portrayal of a bantam, is registered in the
United States Patent Office and in other countries. Marca Registrada.
Bantam Books, Inc., 271 Madison Avenue, New York, N.Y. 10016.*

PRINTED IN THE UNITED STATES OF AMERICA

This book is dedicated to all Democrats and Republicans in this country, who have created the atmosphere which makes the book necessary!

ACKNOWLEDGMENTS

My preparation of this manuscript would not have been possible without the diligent efforts and tireless support of Attorney William Higgs, James Sanders, Arthur Steuer, Walter Glanze, Mike Wately, Robert P. Walker—President of the American Program Bureau, Boston, Massachusetts—Joseph Howell, Steve Rose and Jim McGraw.

I am particularly grateful to Attorney Ruby Burrows, whose thorough research and incisive interpretation of contemporary affairs have provided me with immeasurable background information and insight.

Finally, I want to extend a special word of thanks to my family—my wife, Lillian, and the kids, Michelle, Lynne, Pamela, Paula, Stephanie, Gregory and Gregory. Their tolerance of a husband and father's long periods of absence and their complete support of my many struggles have been an unutterable source of inspiration and courage. They will indeed bring a new dignity to the White House!

DICK GREGORY

CONTENTS

and Physical Abuse . . . The New Black Man . . . The Cop and the Hunter . . . Political Agitators and Ghetto Revolutionaries . . . Calculated Revolution . . . Cancel the Flight

FOREWORD

It is difficult for me to offer visions of a political platform so soon after the assassination of my friend Dr. Martin Luther King, Jr. His death exposes America as the violent nation it is. People the world over have seen this undeniable truth about life in America. Yet America is ironically honored in the eyes of a grateful world for having been the birthplace of such a man as Dr. King. It seems unbelievable that such a violent nation could have sired the world's greatest apostle of peace, love and brotherhood.

America's obsession with violence was exemplified by the events immediately following Dr. King's death. President Johnson was unable to attend the funeral because he had to meet his generals and talk about killing people in Vietnam. While he lived, Martin Luther King never tired of exposing such hypocrisy.

But Martin Luther King walked thousands of miles to make the Constitution of the United States a working reality for *all* Americans. He believed in the Constitution and demanded that it be made to work right once and for all. I share Dr. King's Constitutional obsession; it is a major reason for declaring my own Write-In candidacy.

The life and death of Martin Luther King, Jr., leaves a tormenting question hovering over America: Can a nation whose civil rights are so clearly defined and so loosely interpreted be expected to survive?

WRITE ME IN!

EXECUTIVE ORDERS

A lot of people ask me what is the first thing I would do if I became President of the United States. I thought everyone knew the first thing I would do is paint the White House Black.

The next thing I would do is to bring all the soldiers back from Vietnam and send LBJ . . . with nothing to defend himself with but a barbecue gun . . . I can just see the headlines now: "Twenty Vietcong Slapped in the Mouth with a Barbecued Rib."

I haven't decided on all my Presidential appointments yet. Of course all White House dinner invitations will be handled by Eartha Kitt.

I'll have to be honest with you. When I become President, I'm definitely going to have a colored cook. Somehow I just can't picture a French chef fixing mustard greens, red beans and rice.

When I get into office, I am going to issue an Executive Order to stop selling anything to Rhodesia—except tuna fish, cranberry sauce, cigarettes and color television sets.

Another thing I would do is send all Negroes back to Africa. Before Red China drops that bomb on us . . . A lot of white folks tell me that's unfair. I think it *would* be unfair if it weren't for certain circumstances. Do you realize we have spent billions of dollars in this country for fallout shelters and none of them are located in Negro neighborhoods? If they ever start droppin' those big bombs, we've got to run all the way downtown . . . That's why we're going to Washington and demand that the President either build fallout shelters in black communities or give us a three-day warning . . . If you white folks look around this summer and see a whole lot of colored folks slippin' downtown, they either know something or are just rehearsing.

People ask me, "If you were elected President, what group of people do you think you would have the most trouble with?" And I have no doubt that I would have the most trouble with colored folks. One of my first programs would be to wipe out the poverty program and set up a 55 billion dollar a year White Folks Rest Program. I'd take all those white folks off their good jobs and put them on my Rest Program. And I'd give my black brother a good job for the first time in his life. I guarantee you that after six months of doing this, colored folks would be marching on me at the White House, saying, "What's wrong with you? Lettin' these white folk lay around not working, getting relief checks, havin' all them babies . . ."

Chapter I

WHY I WANT TO BE PRESIDENT

The world has many times been governed by black rulers. Such periods of history have rarely been times of tyranny. The kings of Babylon and the pharaohs of Egypt were black. Saul, the King of Israel, was a black man; as is Haile Selassie. There have been black kings of Greece and sultans of Persia; emperors of Rome; dukes and courtesans of Venice and Spain. Aesop, the father of literature, was black, as was Aesculapius, the father of science. There have been black popes and black presidents.

So as you read this book, and the idea that I just might become President of these United States begins to sink in, please try to remember the words of the Book of Ecclesiastes which suggest that there is really nothing new under the sun.

I grew up in the ghetto of St. Louis and like any other kid in my neighborhood, I heard the myths and unconsciously knew the realities of life's possibilities for a black child in America. Some of my little black neighbors aspired to be doctors, lawyers or teachers. But I dreamed of being a champion; of shattering the myths; of breaking through the cruel and accepted system and creating new realities. Even then I knew that some day I would run for the nation's highest office. For I dared to believe the popular American myth, which stirs the imaginative fantasies of every boy in America, that anyone can become President of the United States.

I did become a champion on the track field in high school and in college. Later I rose to the top of my chosen field of entertainment and joined the galaxy of stars in show business. I achieved fame and fortune, both childhood ambitions, which were seen to be meaningless once attained. I learned early in life the corruption of the capitalistic system. Capitalism respects only wealth, not human values. I was making big money and I was "respected." In reality, my money was respected and I was only tolerated.

My fame and status as a well known entertainer led me into the struggle for human dignity and my fortune was dedicated to that cause. In this great struggle I have had the good fortune to meet other champions, not famous and certainly not wealthy. But champions just the same. There have been many black champions in the sports arena and many black stars in show business. But the real champion, I have come to understand, is the man who has risen to the crest of life's highest purpose— singular and complete devotion to serving one's fellow man. And I have always believed that the nation's highest office *should* represent life's highest purpose.

Politicians and Statesmen

But unfortunately this is not the case in America today. The elective process in the United States is a political enterprise of the worst kind. It breeds politicians rather than statesmen. There is a big difference between politicians and statesmen. Politics means the art of compromise. Most politicians are all-too-well schooled in this art. They compromise to get nominated; they compromise to get elected; and they compromise time and time again, after they are elected, to stay in office. In times of crisis, the politician flexes his muscle. During these next few months, you will see other Presidential candidates flexing their muscles, twisting arms politically to get delegate votes at the party conventions or offering the dividends of political appointment for delivering the vote in November.

The statesman, on the other hand, flexes his mind in times of crisis. Like myself he is a dreamer, with a vision of the very best life has to offer and a determination to see all men have their rightful share of this offering; not as a reward, but because justice will tolerate nothing less. The statesman's devotion is to humanity, to the alleviation of suffering, to the creation of a decent and peaceful human environment throughout the world. The statesman cannot compromise with what he knows to be right, nor can he make any political deals which will allow a form of evil or injustice to be even temporarily victorious. These are indeed times of crisis in America. Lest there be the slightest doubt in the mind of any voter, I am serving notice *now* that I will be a statesman and not a politician.

People will quite naturally ask my qualifications to be President of the United States. Black people in this country have been told all their lives that they could not have a certain job because they were not qualified or lacked the proper training and education. We black folks are used to taking phony tests which have nothing to do with the job for which we are applying. So just *what are* the qualifications for the Presidency and what is the proper training for that responsibility?

The Constitution of the United States lists only two qualifications. A candidate must be a natural-born citizen of the United States and must have reached the age of thirty-five. To illustrate how carefully I planned my childhood dream: I was thirty-five years old October 12, 1967.

The Constitution says nothing of color, sex or education as Presidential qualifications. However, I attended Southern Illinois University. But I shudder to think that a college education qualifies a man for public office. After all, Lyndon Johnson, George Wallace and Ross Barnett are all college men! And to my knowledge, there is not a college in this country which teaches "Presidentology."

Only One Qualification

The one basic qualification for the Presidency, which the Constitution does not mention, but which I feel is supremely important, is a sensitivity to human need. If I must offer qualifications other than constitutional mandate, let them be in the area of my sensitivity to human problems. I was born and raised in the ghetto and have continued to walk those crowded streets of suffering though I no longer live there. I have shared the pain of my black brothers and sisters in the midst of violent and bloody revolt. During the 1965 uprising in Watts, I was shot and the scar of that bullet wound is a lasting reminder of the sorrow the actions of *insensitive politicians* can inflict.

I have spanned the world to voice a plea for peace among men. I have had the good fortune to talk with the common people of this earth, from the Russian worker in Moscow to the poor sharecropper in the rural outposts of Mississippi. I have broken bread in shacks where even bread was a luxury. And I have dined in luxurious restaurants where the bill for a single dinner would feed a Mississippi family for a month. I have marched and protested against injustice with all kinds of people—Indians, locked hopelessly and helplessly in their reservations; suburban whites, painfully victimized by their own social system; ghetto and rural blacks for whom freedom is an increasingly empty word and justice is an unknown commodity. I have shared the secret hopes and the fondest dreams of them all and I have learned that the moral revolution in America is not a fight of blacks against whites; it is a united struggle of right against wrong.

I dropped out of college just short of graduation, because I became convinced that education was not the key to success. A man is born with all the wisdom he needs to gain respect. He does not need a college degree to show human compassion. Respect should never be based upon what a man knows, but rather upon the quality of life he lives. Therefore, I chose to reject any possible link with a system which would respect a man's college degree but not the man himself.

So I will be one of the few Presidents of the United States without a college degree and the candidate of all those Americans who never went to college. To my black brother in the ghetto I can say we are in the same "uneducated" boat together. And to the college professor I can say I have participated in your educational system long enough to know well its limitations.

The Country and the College

But my college days did give me a clue as to how to run the country. I would run this country much the same as a good college president runs his educational institution. The wise college president does not have to be a specialist in all the fields his college teaches. He does not have to be a sociologist to realize that he must seek out the best available man in that field to head his sociology department. Nor does he have to be trained in chemistry to understand how important it is to find the best possible chemist to head his chemistry department. The enlightened college president does not choose his department heads from the list of highest donors to the college!

The President of the United States does not need to be a specialist in knowing how to solve all the world and domestic problems he will face. But he must have wisdom enough to realize that solving problems will depend upon obtaining the best-trained minds in the world to work on the solution. You would not hire a politician to head the space program; you would hire a trained scientist. Nor will a sensible President appoint a politician to head programs designed to eradicate the evils of the ghetto. He will find the best technicians in the world—sociologists, psychiatrists, architects, urban planners and so on—and put them to work on the solution.

The statesman will naturally surround himself with such men, because he is more concerned with the solution to human problems than personal obligation to political colleagues. The politician, on the other hand, will surround himself with those to whom he owes favors, those who have helped him flex his political muscle. Real solutions to actual human problems become secondary considerations. We have witnessed the results of such compromising insanity in Watts, Detroit, Newark, and in city after city which exploded in violent outrage resulting from the insane assassination of Dr. Martin Luther King, Jr.

I have declared my Presidential candidacy in the exhilarating joy of carrying my childhood dream a step further. I want to believe that many Americans prefer the mind of a statesman to the muscle of a politician. I want to believe that a champion of human dignity can become the leader of this nation. I want to believe that the fondest dreams of the human family can be embodied in the office of the Presidency. I want to enter the public forum of debate this election year of 1968, during which the destiny of mankind might very well be decided. I want to be a part of this Presidential race as I have tried to be a meaningful part of so many human causes in the past. This is one demonstration I don't want to miss!

Perhaps most of all, I want the dream of every little black kid in this nation to be strengthened and nurtured by seeing his Mommy and Daddy wearing a button saying "Dick Gregory for President."

I'm not too worried about being a Write-In candidate. Of course, the administration will probably put out a rumor that pencils cause cancer.

Believe it or not, my wife is already preparing to move into the White House. She told me the other night that, when we move in, she's going to remove Lady Bird's tulips—and plant some cotton on the White House lawn.

I feel I have a good chance of being elected President. In fact my oldest daughter, Michelle, has already had three proposals of marriage from Army lieutenants.

And I intend to campaign in every state. I can just see myself now down South—waving to crowds from the back of my campaign bus.

My foreign-aid program will mainly consist of sending money and food to needy people in foreign lands—like Mississippi and Alabama.

I was encouraged to announce my candidacy by the fact that we got a couple of colored mayors in the last elections, in Cleveland and Gary. The mayor of Gary, Indiana, Dick Hatcher, I know personally. I was talking to him not long ago and he informed me that he intends to make Gary an all-segregated town. White folks would be kept with white folks and black folks with black folks. He feels white folks would be happier that way . . . up on the reservation.

When I become President, I will order all television networks to hire more Negroes for commercials. I'm getting tired of looking at television and seeing no black folks getting Excedrin headaches . . . and we're the ones who *should* be getting them . . . I'd like just once to see a dove fly into a black ghetto kitchen . . . And if we had that White Knight, who's always running through the white suburbs, we could solve ghetto problems in a week.

I can be elected. People don't realize what progress black people have made in this country. We got our biggest breakthrough in history last year when we got our very own hurricane. Hurricane Beulah.

Chapter II

HOW I WANT TO BE PRESIDENT

"When in the Course of human events it becomes
necessary for one people to dissolve the political bands
which have connected them with another . . ."
              —The Declaration of Independence

In the spirit of the Declaration of Independence, I
have declared myself the independent, Write-In candidate for President for peace and freedom in 1968. I do
so because I take the words of our nation's birth certifi-
cate very seriously. The current course of human events
in this nation has created a situation where it is necessary for people to exert individual, independent action to
dissolve the political bands which unite them with the
two-party system.

The two-party system in America has made a mockery of democracy by denying people any real choice in
determining the candidates who will represent them.
Candidates are selected through the power plays of the
party machine and such political activities produce candidates who will best represent the interests of the political party rather than the common good of all the people.
Writing in *American Government: Democracy at Work*,
Robert White cites the example of a Cook County convention held in Chicago in 1896. He reports that 644 out
of 723 delegates to the convention, or 89 percent, were
ex-convicts (130), saloon keepers (265), persons who
had been on trial for murder (17), of no occupation

(71), political employees (148), or vagrants, ex-prize fighters or gamblers (13)! From such gatherings, future leaders of the nation are born.

Since my home is in Chicago, I am very familiar with the tactics of the political machine in Cook County. In April, 1967, I ran as the independent Write-In candidate for Mayor of Chicago. On election day I discovered that, although pencils had been affixed to the voting machines so my name could be written in, each pencil was tied to a string long enough to be seen underneath the voting machine curtain. Poll watchers could readily and easily determine which voters picked up the pencil to use it. Since I was the only declared Write-In candidate in the election, it was a safe assumption my name was being written in. So the political machine has a way of continuing to exert control whether it chooses a candidate or not.

Political Prostitution

The essence of true democracy is not only the right to vote, but also the right to select your own candidate. To be forced to select between party dominated choices is to have no *real* choice at all. The 1964 Presidential election was a good example. I did not vote in that election because I refused to be the victim of having to choose between the lesser of two evils. The majority of American voters were so busy choosing the lesser of two evils that they ended up putting into office the evil of the evils.

But to vote in such an election is really to have no choice at all. The only real choice possible in 1964 was to exercise the constitutional right *not* to vote. Look at it this way. Suppose you had a choice of marrying one of two women. One woman is a prostitute seven days a week and the other practices her trade only on weekends. If you were interested in choosing the lesser of two evils, you would decide to marry the weekend prostitute. But you really have no choice at all, for whatever decision you make, you still end up being married to a whore!

Incidentally, if I had voted in the 1964 Presidential election, I would have voted for Barry Goldwater. The only thing wrong with Barry Goldwater in 1964 was that he dared to be the more honest of the two candidates.

For a voter to Write In a candidate of his own choosing represents the best instincts of the democratic process and serves to fulfill a citizen's constitutional rights. It is precisely because of my desire to see a full and complete implementation of the Constitution in this country that I am calling for a Write-In vote on my behalf. I have extended no personal effort to have my name listed on any ballots, though some local groups have taken such action and my name will be listed in some states. My appeal is to each individual voter to exercise his own private and personal constitutional right to write his own ballot and to choose his own candidate, completely free of the choices made by the two-party system.

The idea of writing in a candidate's name seems strange at first, especially in those states where voting machines are used in elections. But it is only because the voting machine symbolizes the computerized corruption of the democratic process that the idea of a Write-In vote seems outrageous. During the more democratic days of America's history, before the two-party system became definitive of the political process, *all* candidates were Write-Ins. The earliest ballots were blank pieces of paper on which the voter wrote the name of the candidate of his choice. Thomas Jefferson, Abraham Lincoln and a host of other folklore heroes were Write-In candidates. And in this decade voters have befuddled the pollsters and frustrated the political parties by writing in candidates in Presidential primary elections.

During the first forty or fifty years of America's history, voting was cast by voice (viva voce) or by standing up to be counted. Each eligible voter made an open declaration of his choice. Such a voting method was extremely open to corruption, and secret ballots were a necessary reform. Voters declaring their open choice were vulnerable to intimidation and reprisal and the secret ballot was one way of counteracting these repressive measures in the interest of true democracy.

Today the corruption and intimidation is of a different sort. The corrosion of democracy begins before the ballot is drawn up, in the smoke-filled backrooms of political conventions. And the corrosion continues when the right to vote is mocked by representatives of the party machine intimidating voters to get them to "vote right." Today as never before it is necessary to *break* the political bands which tie voters to party politics and to call for an open declaration of voter sentiment through a creative use of the secret ballot.

Peace and Freedom

I offer myself as the independent candidate of all Americans who want to make their own declaration of independence this election year. I am issuing a call for a Write-In vote to all my fellow citizens who share my dream for America; whose concern for their country is greater than party loyalty; whose desire to solve the tremendous world and social problems confronting the soul of this nation supersedes an allegiance to a party platform.

To rid this nation of political and moral decay we must create an independent army of determined voters who will march to the polls in November and emerge victorious. During America's World Wars, the designation "Democrat" or "Republican" had no meaning to the soldier on the front line of battle. Party labels are irrelevant to the defense of democracy. And the defense of democracy at home, in America's own political life, requires front-line soldiers who refuse to accept party labels or choices and who wage a just war according to their own strategies.

There are a variety of possible strategies. Each independent action should be designed to create a real alternative to the stale and decadent dominance of the two-party system. The use of *pencil power* and the creation of a personal, individual ballot of one's own choosing is one strategy. The current emergence of an active Peace and Freedom party in many states throughout the country is another. The creation of such a third party, a party based on the magnificent dream and the human aspiration of peace and freedom, exposes the shallow aspirations of the two-party system. Such a party offers a public forum for the expression of moral concern and provides a means of organizing those whose dream of democracy will not submit to or be stifled by current political realities. Any political strategy which makes possible the public exposure of the dreams of statesmen rather than the calculated partial commitments of politicians receives my wholehearted endorsement.

This is how I want to be President. I want to assume office in January of 1969 as the result of a political battle waged by an independent army of voters determined to save this great democracy and to save America from herself. Whatever the outcome of the vote in November, the waging of the battle is victory in itself. If I should happen to fail to receive the majority of that vote, I will still be the commander-in-chief of an independent voting army and will declare myself their President-in-Exile. That army will continue to wage war for justice and dignity among men for years to come.

My Government-in-Exile would operate side-by-side with the other government in America. I will have my own Inaugural Ball on the evening of January 21st, though the music and food will probably differ from the other President's celebration. I will deliver my own State of the Union address on the same evening the other President delivers his message before a joint session of Congress. Whenever the occupant of the White House fails to respond to the just demands of human need, the independent army will bring their concerns to the Black

House to their President-in-Exile. The new Government-in-Exile will offer political asylum to every man, woman and child in America who is devoted to freedom and true democracy. Ours will be an active exile, a functioning government and a marching army. For the first time since the Declaration of Independence, the voice of true democracy will be heard.

BLACK ON WHITE

Some white folks I just can't understand. They're more concerned about busing a kid to school than they are about shipping a kid to Vietnam . . . That's like worrying about dandruff when you've got cancer of the eyeballs.

I can't believe how many white folks are silly enough to think that if black folks took over the country in the morning, we'd make slaves out of them . . . Now don't get me wrong, we would *like* to . . . But think of the tremendous hardship it would be for black folks to make all white folks slaves . . . Do you know what that means? It means that every black cat in America would have twelve white folks to feed for the rest of his life . . . I can just see it now. A black cat would ask me, "Greg, are you going to Europe again this summer?" And I'd answer, "Hell, no, man. I've got to get seven more jobs to feed these damn white folks" . . . Why, it would take us 2½ years to just teach white folks to eat watermelon right . . . And if we made slaves out of all white folks, it'd be the best thing that ever happened to them. With 180 million white folks in this country, they'd pick all the cotton in two days . . . Then they'd have 363 days just to sit around and rest . . . learn them songs . . . plot revolt.

Of course, as President of the United States I'll have a white chauffeur. And I guess you know I'm going to sit in the front. . . . And I figure it will cost me a pretty penny to get a steering wheel long enough for this white cat to drive from the back of the car.

A lot of people have asked me what I think about that black cat in South Africa giving the white cat his heart for a transplant. I say it was a great gesture. I hope all white folks realize that out of all heart transplants, his is the only one that made it . . . I don't mean to imply anything, but I do hope you white folks don't assume that we're going to end up being your spare parts . . . Of course, I think it proved to a lot of people that colored folks have rhythm in something else other than their feet . . . And it also proved to all those white folks that don't want colored folks living next door to them that deep down in their hearts, they know we're right.

Chapter III

THIS NATION IS INSANE

America is faced with a pollution crisis. Air and water pollution are making our land uninhabitable. In New York City just breathing the air has the cancer-producing benzpyrene equivalent to smoking two packages of cigarettes a day. It is claimed that air pollution was responsible for 80 percent of the rise in deaths from respiratory diseases from 1930 to 1960. Chemicals and pesticides in the atmosphere are exterminating both pests and people and there are currently approximately 20 tons of DDT in the bodies of the American people.

This year, the 90 million motor vehicles in use will burn an estimated 60 billion gallons of gasoline, or about 700 gallons for the typical automobile. This means that each automobile in the country will discharge in a single year over 1,600 pounds of carbon monoxide, 230 pounds of hydrocarbons, and 77 pounds of oxides of nitrogen. Fifty million Americans will drink water that does not meet Public Health Service drinking water standards and an additional 45 million Americans will drink water that has not been tested.

The murky, congested air destroys crops, from $6 to $10 million annually in California alone, corrodes machinery, raises cleaning costs and may make milk unmarketable which comes from cows breathing polluted, DDT filled air.

But the number one problem facing this country today is not air and water pollution. It is *moral pollution*. That

America is totally infected with moral pollution is demonstrated by this nation's preoccupation with violence. I am often questioned about talking about violence when I am supposed to be nonviolent. For the record, I *am* nonviolent. I am a nonviolent, vegetarian pacifist. But there is no way to honestly assess the American social and political scene and not speak of violence. America is a very, very violent country. Matt Dillon comes into American homes every week teaching citizens that it is a virtue to shoot straight. The United States Constitution gives a man the right to carry a gun in his home. We are indeed a violent nation.

Though I am committed to nonviolence, I do not force my philosophy on anyone else. There is nothing any man can do to me to make me kill him or inflict personal injury upon him. But that is my own personal hang-up. I do not preach nonviolence as the only alternative. I am a vegetarian because I do not believe animals should be killed, but I will never knock a steak out of another person's hand. Because I am known to be nonviolent, every summer when the riot season begins people call me asking if I will come and "cool the black folks off." I didn't heat them up and I am not going anywhere to cool them off!

Nonviolence Is a Fraud

The American tragedy is the perverse distortion of the concept of nonviolence. Nonviolence in this country means that I am not supposed to hit an American white man. But I can go all over the world shooting people and get medals for it. If every Negro in this country stood up and said, "I am nonviolent," America would love us. But if we tried to show America that nonviolence means we are not supposed to be violent under any circumstances, *anywhere* in the world, which means, of course, not going to war, we would be called "Communists" and thrown in jail. Nonviolence in this country is a fraud.

The late Dr. Martin Luther King, Jr., was a close personal friend of mine. He was probably the greatest moral force on the face of the earth. Yet I did not appreciate even Dr. King telling black folks to be nonviolent and not telling white folks the same thing. And I would feel the same if white folks were exercising their constitutional right of marching in the Negro community. I would be equally upset if white folks were being attacked by my black brothers and Dr. King told whites to turn the other cheek and didn't impose the same standards upon blacks. I believe the world would be a better place to raise our children if *all* men were nonviolent. We should begin teaching nonviolence on a mass scale rather than just teaching it to one segment of the world population. My personal commitment to nonviolence is total and means I could not join my black brothers in Africa were they to rise in bloody revolt. Nonviolence prohibits killing as a means of expressing even the most just of grievances.

The supreme hypocrisy of America is that this nation is not disturbed by white violence. But it is scared to death of black violence. This common bond of fear was very evident in the State of the Union address of January, 1968. At that time it was almost impossible to get the Senate, the Congress and the President to agree on anything. Yet there was instantaneous agreement when the President said, "The American people have had enough of rising crime and lawlessness in this country." Everyone stood and cheered for five minutes when that issue was mentioned. Why? Because "crime in the streets" is America's new way of saying "nigger."

Do not think for one minute that I am saying black crime should go unchecked; that it shouldn't be dealt with. I am merely asking at what point the citizens of this sick, insane nation will become equally upset over white crime! When I see the President, of all people, talking about crime in the streets I am insulted. He went to Congress in his late twenties, a poor, humble school teacher.

Today he is a millionaire. But nobody asks where his money came from. If he were black, everyone would *demand* to know. Bobby Baker worked for the President and stole $8 million. Can the American people be sick enough to believe that the President didn't get any of that money? If Bobby Baker had worked for Adam Clayton Powell, both of them would be in jail.

What day will we have a President who will face the nation on television and not only vow to wipe out crime in the street, but also will pledge to wipe out the crime syndicate in America. Perhaps that doesn't count. Perhaps the crime syndicate is too white to upset anyone. If black folks *took over* the crime syndicate, it would be wiped out in a week.

America is insane and irrational when considering black crime. When a nation becomes more upset over a purse snatcher than a narcotics dealer, that nation is out of its mind. Looting and arson in the ghettos have produced a national cry for law and order. Yet think of all the bodies the crime syndicate has stuffed in the trunks of automobiles and all of the people machine-gunned in the streets. There has yet to be a national cry of moral outrage demanding an end to syndicate rule of major cities.

In that same State of the Union address, the President asked for appropriations to hire a hundred Assistant District Attorneys and a hundred FBI agents to control the traffic in LSD. The President mentioned LSD by name, but he didn't refer to heroin or reefers. Why? Because the syndicate controls heroin and reefers. And when the crime syndicate controls LSD, it won't be mentioned in a State of the Union address either.

America is more concerned with its problem of crime in the streets than with its involvement in crime all over the world. It is ironic to consider our illegal and lawless actions in Vietnam. The demand for law and order at home should be matched by a respect for law and order abroad. When the criminal speaks of how he is going to solve crime, this nation is in deep trouble.

No, I am not saying that violent black folks should not be stopped. Nor am I saying their dynamite and molotov cocktails should not be confiscated. But I *am* asking that this nation give equal attention to the Minutemen who are stockpiling weapons out in the white suburbs. All of the ammunition and dynamite the Minutemen have doesn't seem to bother America.

America will only become concerned over the Minutemen when it is discovered that they are going to kill white folks and not black folks. That discovery will upset the entire nation. The Minutemen have not shot any black folks yet. You couldn't give a Minuteman a million dollars and a tank and get him to go to Harlem! If the Minutemen's dynamite buried in the lily-white suburbs ever blows up one night accidentally, it will wipe out whole blocks of white folks. Then America will become concerned.

The Double Standard

There is an insane double standard to America's violence. In Orangeburg, South Carolina, three black kids were killed on the college campus. The slaughter was rationalized and justified by saying the students were unruly. For the past ten years white college kids have been going to Fort Lauderdale, Florida, every spring and tearing up the town. Not one of them has ever been shot. I am not saying "Start shooting white folks to justify killing black folks." Nor am I saying this country cannot kill black folks. I am just warning you that the nation had better prepare itself to understand our attitude after black folks are killed.

Consider what it means for police to shoot into a college campus. Have you ever read where the police shot into a whorehouse, or gunned down a group of pimps standing on the street corner? When the Mafia had its big meeting in Apalachin, New York, the police didn't shoot into the meeting room. But they will shoot into a group of black college kids and think nothing of it.

Understand the insult of America's double standard. Muhammad Ali has lost his world heavyweight championship title *before* he goes to jail. But Jimmy Hoffa didn't lose his job until he was placed behind bars. Senator Dodd still has his job, but Adam Clayton Powell lost his congressional seat. That is an insult and black folks are angry.

Moral pollution has affected America's ability to tell the truth. I would rather say lying represents a basic immorality than give it a sweet-sounding name like "credibility gap." When Dwight Eisenhower was President a U-2 plane was shot down. Our national leader went on television talking about "U-what?" Ike said he never heard of the U-2 plane. The terrifying element in the U-2 incident is not so much that Ike lied, but that this nation is sick enough to have gone to war over that lie. Our ambassador sat in the United Nations denying that we had U-2 flights, while the Russians sat right next to him assembling the parts. Not to mention that they had the pilot.

Or take the Pueblo incident. The President came on television and said that the Pueblo was twenty miles out on international waters. The next day he said it was sixteen miles out. Finally he got it down to twelve miles. I expect to pick up the paper any day and see where the Pueblo had dropped anchor!

Racism—Black and White

There is a terrible racist strain to the moral pollution in America. Americans must wake up and realize that we are the most racist country in the world, including South Africa. South Africa does not have a United States Constitution pretending that all people have equal opportunities under the law. Many times white folks get upset when they hear a black man talk about racism. If you reacted in such a manner to my accusation, it is an illustration of the racism in your own mind. I did not say that American white folks were the world's leading racists; I said America is a racist country. Unlike the National Advisory Commission on Civil Disorders report, I do not speak of white racism in America. I speak of racism—black and white. Whether you want to admit it or not, black folks are Americans too. Anyone who has been born and raised in this country cannot escape infection with racism, be he black or white. This white society is so frightened to realize that black folks are racists as well as white folks. It shouldn't be surprising. We learned it from white folks. We've been watching them for four hundred years.

When Stokely Carmichael said that he didn't want white folks in the civil rights movement any longer, some racist press cried "reverse racism." There is nothing reverse about it. Black folks have a right to hate white folks the same as white folks have a right to hate us. No black man is going through the back door to throw a brick at white folks.

The statement of Stokely Carmichael was one of the most purely moral and honest statements ever to come out of the civil rights movement. And there was nothing racist about it. His statement pertained to local situations —Georgia, Alabama and Mississippi. Yet he was completely misunderstood. To be honest, I am glad his statement was misunderstood. It has rendered a great service to the movement. People who insist, both white and black, that Stokely is losing friends for the movement were not needed in the movement in the first place.

People who have left the movement because of the statements of Stokely Carmichael were looking for a way out anyway. Most Americans are so far away from the civil rights movement that they are as misinformed about it as they are about Vietnam. If the closest you get to the

movement is what you read in the press, you really cannot understand. And if you can believe what you read
in the papers about Vietnam, you can believe anything.

But people left the movement willingly and blamed
their departure on Stokely's statement. Since when has
Stokely Carmichael had such power over white folks that
they will do anything he tells them to do? When he says,
"We don't want white folks in the movement," they
scurry to leave. But if Stokely had said, "I want all white
folks in America to get up at six o'clock every morning
for the next ten years and give half their paycheck to the
civil rights movement," would they have done that?

Stokely Carmichael's statement was simple. He was
saying we are tired of all those young northern white kids
coming down South with all their hang-ups and their
guilt, bugging our redneck Mississippi crackers, when
they couldn't take a Negro home with them in the suburbs of Detroit, Chicago, Cleveland or Los Angeles. All
Stokely was saying was: "Before you come down South
and bug your redneck cracker cousin, take a Negro home
with you and bug your own Momma." And after you've
dealt with your own Momma and Daddy, come on down
South and march on your racist cousin. When you see
that Mississippi redneck reacting, you will realize that
not too long ago you saw your Momma and Daddy reacting in the same way. Then maybe you will have a little
bit more compassion for your southern white brother!

The fact that America is the number one most racist
country in the world is nothing for Americans to be
ashamed of. No one alive in America today had anything
to do with creating the racism which exists. We inherited
it. The thing that amazes me is that in 1968 America
refuses to admit that racism exists and seems to be obsessed with trying to cover up or deny it. But it is hard
to conceal. Julius Hobson pointed out, in an article for
the Saturday Evening Post, that Uncle Sam is a bigot.
Citing the Civil Service Commission's *Study of Minority
Group Employment in the Federal Government* (1966),

Hobson showed that 88 percent of all the federally employed black people were in the lowest paying jobs, even though they were career employees and ostensibly on the merit system.

Many white people reacted to Stokely's statement about white folks in the movement by saying, "Why are you Negroes so hard on northern white liberals?" The answer is because they are obsolete. We do not need a crowd in the civil rights movement. We merely need a few sincere, committed, honest people. We don't need northern white liberals anymore. We need northern white radicals. If liberals want to continue their old style of operation, let them go up to the Indian reservation. The Indian needs liberals. Let the liberals go out into the fields and help the Mexican-American. He needs liberals. But if they do as good a job for the Indians and the Mexican-Americans as they have done for us, I guarantee the liberals will be obsolete on the reservations and in the fields too. Selma, Alabama, placed the liberal attitude in focus. Former Illinois Senator Paul Douglas' wife marched courageously across the bridge on that first day of confrontation with the police. But when we were marching in Chicago later that year for open housing and school integration, we couldn't find her anywhere.

Moral pollution seems to have infected the mind of America and brought the nation to the brink of insanity. We see the marks of insanity all around us. For four months in 1967 the papers reported every day congressional debates on whether or not the nation should have a Clean Meat Bill. Is that insanity or not? I could understand Premier Kosygin not wanting Americans to have clean meat. And I can understand the Vietcong not wanting us to have any meat at all. But it is unbelievable that our representatives debated four months on whether or not their constituents should have clean meat. The most insane act came later. I picked up the paper one day and read the headline: "Congress Reaches a Compromise on a Clean Meat Bill."

Now I am a vegetarian, so it is understandable that I can't fathom what a compromise on clean meat might be. It says to me that Americans can't eat clean meat and they can't eat dirty meat. I ask all meat-eaters, "Does your meat taste different lately?" Such political debate illustrates a nation which has lost its mind.

Stokely Carmichael and Rap Brown symbolize the national insanity. Stokely is twenty-seven years old and Rap is twenty-four. Yet these two young men have scared the most mighty nation on the face of this earth to death. Such a nation must be insane. Do you remember when former Russian Premier Khrushchev said he was going to "bury" us? And he had the means to back up his statement. Our response as a nation was to say, "C'mon, baby, we're ready." We weren't scared of Khrushchev and Russia, but we are afraid of Stokely and Rap. Stokely doesn't have one missile. Rap Brown doesn't have a canoe, to say nothing of a Navy!

The Tiger and the Cricket

In her insane fear, America tells black folks to be nonviolent. After the assassination of Dr. Martin Luther King, white America said: "Remember the memory of Dr. King and be nonviolent." White America owns all the guns, the tanks, makes all the napalm, builds all the missiles, owns all the nuclear vessels, has an Army and a Navy, controls the FBI and the CIA, the local police, the state police and the National Guard. Yet white America can look at black folks, who do not manufacture one gun, and tell them to be nonviolent.

To me that is like the tiger telling the cricket to be nonviolent. The cricket looked up at the tiger one day and said, "Please, Mr. Tiger, get your foot off me." The tiger looked down and said, "Boy, you'll never live to see the day when I'll take my foot off you. But I won't have my foot on your kids." And the cricket answered, "If you don't take your foot off now, and let me get over to my wife, there won't be any kids. Please," the cricket pleaded, "Take your foot off me."

The tiger answered angrily, "Shut up, cricket, and be nonviolent." The cricket got to thinking. One day he said to himself, "If the tiger keeps telling me to be nonviolent, I must have something going for me that I don't know about. Let me find out what it is."

So the cricket struggled loose and jumped up on the tiger's back. The tiger rolled over on the ground. When the cricket felt the full weight of the tiger, he said: "It must not be that." Next he jumped on the tiger's head and the tiger butted his head up against the tree. The cricket was ready to give up. Giving it one last try, the cricket jumped into the tiger's ear. And the cricket used the only weapon he had. In the tiger's ear he said: "Chirp-chirp, chirp-chirp."

The tiger went crazy. That same tiger who told the cricket to be nonviolent forgot to be nonviolent himself. He got so upset over the cricket being in his ear that the tiger took his paw and with one swift stroke he hit his own ear trying to silence the cricket. But the blow was so mighty, he knocked his head off.

Then the cricket came out of the tiger's ear. He looked at the tiger laying there and said, "Mr. Tiger should have been nonviolent."

White America is the tiger and black America is the cricket. All Stokely Carmichael and Rap Brown did was to get in the ear of white America and make some noise. And it looks like white America will make the same mistake the tiger made. She is going to forget to be nonviolent. She is coming into the black ghettos with tanks and heavy ammunition. With a might blow she intends to silence the voice of black America.

But white America forgets that there is a lot of sewer and natural gas underneath those ghettos. The same pipes which carry gas to white folks' ovens service black folks' ovens. If a shell from one of those tanks hits a sewer or a pipeline and ignites the gas, a whole town will go up in flames and white and black will burn together.

I hope America does not follow the path of the tiger. If the tiger had followed his own advice, he would have lived. And if America demands nonviolence but fails to practice it, she will surely die.

A morally polluted America fears the truth. The CIA followed Stokely Carmichael all over the world. They heard every speech he gave, yet they were never able to report back home that he lied about America. We have all read the statements of both Stokely Carmichael and Rap Brown and not once can we honestly say that they have lied about this nation. It is a terrifying thought that a whole nation despises two men for telling the truth. When that happens, there is nothing wrong with those two men; but there is something terribly wrong with that nation.

The Corrupt American History Book

Moral pollution is written deep in the record of America's history. I am glad America forced me to read her corrupt history book. And I am glad she continues to insist that black kids in the ghetto read it. When I was a kid, I didn't want to read American history. I went to an all-black, segregated high school in St. Louis and I knew the United States Constitution did not apply to me. Our high school was so black we didn't even have white mice in the research department.

Oh, that first page of the American history book is beautiful. I cry when I read it. It tells of a man who wanted relief from the yoke of oppression of the King and the Queen. He longed for a new land where he could have freedom of speech, freedom of expression and the opportunity to worship God in his own way. Yes, that first page of American history is beautiful.

But don't turn the page. The story quickly becomes morally polluted. It says that, on his way to find his freedom and to worship his God, the pilgrim stole US.

How is a man on his way to finding freedom going to start his new free existence with some slaves? It is a strange man who seeks relief from oppression by enslaving a group of people whom he later condemns for seeking relief.

And as you turn the pages of that American history book, the story gets more and more polluted. The pilgrim lands in the New World and discovers a land that is already occupied. How do you find something that somebody else already has and you claim you discovered it? And we talk about crime in the streets!

That is like my wife and I walking down the street and seeing you and your wife sitting in your brand-new automobile. Suppose my wife says to me, "Gee, I'd like to have a car like that." And I answer, "Let's discover it." So I walk over to you and your wife and say, "Get out of that damned car. My wife and I just discovered it." The shock and surprise you would naturally feel gives you some idea of how the Indians must have felt.

The double standard in America fails to appreciate American history. White America idolizes Patrick Henry and condemns Rap Brown. But Rap Brown has only dared to become as bitter as Patrick Henry. When Patrick Henry said, "Give me Liberty or give me Death," he was not talking about singing freedom songs to the British. Nor was he talking about going to Boston to help them unload their tea. He was talking about *doing that thing*.

Rap Brown said, "Get a gun, black folks, and watch the police." And white America went crazy. But in the American history book you find that statement wasn't original. Paul Revere rode through the white community and said, "Get a gun, white folks, the British are coming." At that point in history, the British were the police.

Our nation's treasured Declaration of Independence clearly states that where rights and privileges are denied by a government over long periods of time it is a man's duty to abolish that government. Malcolm X did not write that document. Stokely, Rap and SNCC didn't have a thing to do with it. Perhaps the founding fathers made a basic mistake when they drafted the Declaration of Independence. They forgot to put "White Only" on it.

When I read the American history book, there is one thing I just cannot believe. It says that George Washington and his ragged band of foreigners conquered the continent and defeated the whole British Army. And why did he do it? The history book says because of a tax on some tea. When I read that it just didn't make sense to me. It must have been over some issue like civil rights, or fair housing, or jobs. But it really was a tax on tea. In 1968, most Americans don't even drink tea! Do you honestly think there is such a difference between white folks and black folks that America can give us a book bursting with pride for a Revolutionary War over a tea tax and yet not see what the black man in the ghetto is getting ready to do?

Try To Understand

White America's violent rebuke of the philosophy of nonviolence made Stokely Carmichael and Rap Brown what they are today. They both began their civil rights careers trying desperately to clean up that American history book and make the Constitution a document of which *all* Americans could be proud. You must understand what they went through when they were just kids, organizers in the South for the Student Non-violent Coordinating Committee. I'll never forget when I first met Stokely Carmichael six years ago in Greenwood, Mississippi. He insulted me. I was new to the movement and Stokely said, "If you can't be nonviolent, get the hell back up North." Many people in this country forget, or perhaps never knew, that it was Rap Brown, Stokely Carmichael and other members of SNCC who taught nonviolence. They taught nonviolence as a strategy while

Martin Luther King had to fly all over the country explaining the concept to white folks. If you could have seen what those kids went through, you would understand what they are talking about now.

I used to watch them guarding their Freedom House in Greenwood, wondering when it was going to be blown up. Do you know what they were guarding it with? Nothing but a nonviolent attitude. You try that sometime. Imagine yourself waiting for someone to come with dynamite and you are sitting there with no defense but a nonviolent attitude; in a country where grown men go hunting little-bitty rabbits with shotguns.

Think what it means to be down South for six years, sleeping on the floor next to your comrades lined up in a row. And one night you notice an empty place in the line. One of your comrades has not come home that night and you know he is dead. The police have run him off the highway and then reported that he was drunk and killed in an auto accident. And you know your comrade never took a drink in his life. The FBI knows how many civil rights workers were killed that were not reported.

Perhaps you would understand Stokely and Rap a little bit better if you had been with us in Birmingham, Alabama. They arrested 2,400 demonstrators and put us in jail. There were many little kids in the group—four, five, six and seven years old. In the southern jails like all other jails they separate the kids from the adults, the little boys from the little girls and, uniquely in the South, blacks from whites. Our cell happened to be across from where they were keeping the little girls; children from four to ten years old. I stayed in that jail four nights and saw what was happening across the way. Can you imagine what it feels like to watch police bring in lesbians and turn them loose on those young kids? Do you know what it is like having to look at a lesbian tamper with a four-year-old kid? I do not write these words to arouse your sympathy. I only want you to know and understand what those SNCC kids have gone through. The FBI knew about these atrocities, but they never made the knowledge public.

Or maybe you should have been with Stokely and Rap in Greenwood when they tried to integrate the schools. All during the summer months, while most Americans were on vacation, they had to canvass the black community. They had to convince poor black sharecroppers that their kids were needed to help integrate the schools. White folks were saying black folks didn't want to integrate. Even though the Supreme Court ruling says the schools must be integrated, the white folks said, the colored people won't show up.

SNCC did a good job that summer. They got twelve families to permit them to use their kids. At least they thought they had twelve when they went to bed the night before the opening day of school. The next morning only eight reported—four had copped out. Do you know what it feels like to go to a five-year-old kid's house to pick him up for school? He is all smiles and happy. And as you place his little black hand in your hand you wonder why someone hasn't had the courage to tell him that he might be going to die.

When you pull up to the school building, you see the cops barricading it and the sheriff says, "Where you going, nigger?" And you say, "I'm going to school." The little kid looks up and says, "Mornin', mister." And the sheriff snaps, "Well, you can't bring that car in here." So you park the car and get out. You tightly grip that little black hand in yours and the inside of your hand is soaking wet with sweat. Not the five-year-old kid's sweat, but your own.

About twenty-five feet away from the building, where you have to turn to go up those stairs, you see something that makes you know that somebody is going to die. When you hit the steps, you know you weren't wrong. You are not only attacked by the mob, but by the sheriff and the police. The next thing you know you are lying in the gutter with that cracker's foot on your chest and a double-barreled shotgun on your throat. And you hear a voice say, "Move, nigger, and I'll blow your brains out." You're terrified but you think how ironic it is that the only time white folks will admit you have brains is when they are talking about what they are going to do to them.

It is a terrifying feeling to look up and realize for the first time that today is your day to die. And you look across the street and see the FBI taking pictures and you know damn well they will never be shown. You know also that if a black man had his foot on that cracker's chest, those pictures would be released for the *Today* show the next morning.

Then the most horrible thing happens that has ever happened to you in your life. You suddenly realize that the little black hand is not there. And you turn around to look for that little five-year-old kid. You spot him just in time to see a brick hit him right in the mouth. It just doesn't read right for some reason. You have to actually see a brick hit a five-year-old kid in the mouth, regardless of what color the kid is. Only then can you realize the depths of blind and insane hate.

You see the look in that little black child's eye. He can't even react like a five-year-old kid should react after being hurt. He can't run to the adults because they are spitting and kicking at him. You see a white mother lean over that little kid and spit on him and stomp at him, but she is filled with so much hate she misses.

Now you have to take that bruised and bleeding little kid, whose early-morning happy smile has been pulverized and perhaps erased forever, back to his parents who entrusted him to you. And you have to try to explain what happened. You have to hope you will have their support when you are ready to try again. Your own words choke you and anything you are able to say sounds so unconvincing.

You may never be able to justify Stokely and Rap, but

when you know what they have been through, you may
be able to understand them. When Stokely and Rap had
faith in America, they were screaming in the dark to a
nation that didn't care. Now they have no faith in America and they jet around in the broad open daylight taking
care of an insane nation. And everyone seems to hear
them now, but they never listened before. If all white
Americans went through the same treatment those
SNCC kids went through, half of them would have committed suicide and the other half would be burning this
insane country to the ground.

Political Psychosis

This country is so insane that it fell victim to psychotic
hysteria over the utterance of two simple little words:
Black Power. The press had a field day condemning the
use of those two words, asking what had happened to
"responsible" Negro leadership. The two words "black"
and "power" were portrayed as the two most filthy words
in the Negro vocabulary. Since when did either of those
words become obscene?

The most obscene two words black folks have used for
the past hundred years are "m.f." Negroes are always
"m.f.'n' " something—m.f. tree or m.f. job. But a white
newspaper never ran an editorial about the use of those
two words. You never heard the New York Times say,
"Why don't Negroes stop using those two words. Mother
is a very sacred word in American society." Yet when we
get two clean words like "black" and "power," which
even the Pope can use, newspapers try to say they are
the most obscene words we ever came across.

Many people are distorted enough to think that "m.f."
is a Negro invention. "That's colored talk," they will say.
We do use "m.f." a lot, but we didn't create the phrase.
White folks started the use of that term. They were
sophisticated enough to say Oedipus Rex and teach
world literature with it.

Our Vietnam policy illustrates the insanity of this nation. America did not even sign the treaty at the Geneva Convention. Yet we are hopelessly involved in Vietnam. If we would work as hard to uphold our treaties with the Indians as we do to defend a treaty we didn't even sign, this could be a groovy country. We go across the world to Vietnam, 10,000 miles away, pretending to do something for a foreign people, yet we have an Indian in this country who is worse off on his reservation than the Vietnamese have ever been.

Why are we in Vietnam? It cannot be to defend democracy as we have continually said. If so, where was America when democracy fell in Greece several months ago? When that happened we ended up recognizing the new government. Can America really be that insane?

The American people are upset over the North Vietnamese, the Vietcong and President De Gaulle. Some American citizens are boycotting wines and other French products. When will the American people become equally upset over the Russians? Most of the ammunition used by the North Vietnamese to kill American boys comes from Russia. But we are not mad at the Russians. We still bring the Russian ballet to this country. We still bring in foreign exchange students from Russia. There are nonstop commercial flights between New York City and Moscow. Yet every time a patriotic, red-blooded American kid is blown out of the sky over North Vietnam, it happens with a Russian missile. Are we really this consistent in our insanity and inconsistent in our hostilities?

America speaks with pride of the fruits of democracy and advocates democracy for the rest of the world. Yet we go all over the world trying to force democracy upon people at gunpoint. If we would make democracy a reality in this country, we could bring our guns home. Something that is really valuable does not have to be forced upon people. If you put $10,000 on your front porch, you will not have to take a gun and force someone

to take it. Just leave the money clearly visible and someone will come along and recognize its advantages.

I have been all over the world, including Moscow,
Russia. And in all my travels I have never met anyone
who was opposed to freedom. I stood on the street corner
in Moscow and talked with the Russian laborers. They
were in favor of freedom. The world is telling America
that it is against *our* form of freedom.

Riots Help the Cause

Our form of freedom is being exposed today by the
riots which are tearing asunder the inner-core of major
American cities. White America insists that riots are
hurting the Negro cause. An illustration of the insanity
of this nation is that riots are *not* hurting our cause.
They have only helped.

Look at it this way. If I snatched a lady's purse and
while I was running away from the scene of the crime
someone snatched that same purse from me, I could not
report the incident to the police because I was wrong
in the first place. It is the same with riots. Since America
was wrong to begin with, riots have only helped the
Negro cause. And this country hates black folks so much
that if riots really were hurting our cause, many white
folks wouldn't tell us.

After the revolt in Detroit, I was hoping that the government would prove to all black folks that rioting is
self-destructive. I was hoping the government would say,
"All right, we're going to show you black folks how we
treat people who behave themselves." I was hoping the
government would reach out a hand to the Indian reservation and set my red brother free, because he has not
been rioting and yet his cause is so just.

If the Indians would get up on a viaduct over a highway one day and start shooting at white folks on their
way home from work, they would get immediate attention. The President would be on national television

that same evening saying, "I want you Indians to know that I am not just the President of the black folks and the white folks. I am the President of the red folks too." He would appoint a top specialist in Indian affairs to meet with the protestors and consider their grievances. And that specialist would probably be some Negro from Chicago.

But America does not even consider the needs of the Indian, even on Thanksgiving, which is a holiday stolen from him. America only understands violence. If the Indians would resurrect the practice of scalping white folks, the justice of his cause would receive nation-wide acceptance.

The admission that riots have helped the black cause is a shameful mark of America's insanity. After Detroit literally burned to the ground, the Ford Motor Company hired 6,000 Negroes in two days' time. There were no phony tests attached to the job applications. For the first time the emphasis was sincerely placed upon actually *hiring* black folks, rather than devising subtle ways to limit their employment. Why the sudden change in emphasis? Because the fires of the summer of 1967 got too close to the Ford plant. Henry Ford thought, "Don't scorch the Mustangs, baby." Do you realize how long it would take to get 6,000 jobs for black folks using the startegy of nonviolent, peaceful demonstration? Colored friends of mine in Detroit tell me there were so many Negroes lined up outside the Ford plant to get one of those 6,000 jobs that you would have thought the plantation was coming back.

White America speaks of the progress the Negro has made in this country and uses it as an excuse to tell black folks to behave themselves. Black folks do not want to hear about progress, especially from white folks. Black folks know who has made progress in this country. When white Americans came to this country, they came as free individuals and they began with a plus five advantage. When black folks came to this country, they came as

slaves and their shackled existence gave them a minus
five disadvantage. Look at the balance sheet today.
White folks are still plus five and black folks have moved
into a position of plus four. Black people still do not
have their freedom, but they have moved up nine digits
to the white folks' none. <u>White America does not qualify
to judge progress in this country.</u>

Who Stinks?

America's form of freedom, the mockery she has
made of democracy, is exposed in the eyes of the world
by the way black people are treated in this country. They
are herded like cattle into the restricted concentration
camps of ghetto life. Los Angeles, California, is a good
example. Statistics show that in Los Angeles proper,
there are 7.5 people per acre of land. In the black area of
Watts, there are 27.9 people per acre. Yet white America
has nerve enough to suggest that Negroes smell and that
their neighborhoods overflow with garbage in the streets.
But if the situation was reversed, and twenty-seven white
folks were herded onto an acre of land, America would
quickly see who stinks!

Under present conditions, black neighborhoods are
quite naturally dirty; for the simple reason that they are
inhumanly overpopulated. For every seven white folks
throwing gum wrappers in the street, there are twenty-
seven black folks doing the same thing. To add insult to
injury, the same number of garbage collectors are sent
into the black community to remove the refuse as are
sent into the white community. One day white folks are
going to find some of that garbage in their own back-
yard. Black people have made up their minds that, if
white folks will not share their garbage collectors fairly
and squarely with them, we black folks will share our
garbage equally with whites!

Even Hitler in his madness had enough sense to realize that the smell of his concentration camps was not "dirty, stinking, property depreciating Jews." He knew when 15,000 people were herded into a concentration camp, it was not Judaism he was smelling. It was pure Nazism. And white America must realize when they see the conditions of filth in the black ghetto, it is America they see and democracy they smell. The day America wants black folks to smell a little better is the day she had better sweeten up democracy for them.

America's insanity speaks of a fair housing bill as if it were a mark of progress. Black people must resent this kind of thinking. When Stalin's daughter, Svetlana Alliluyeva, came to this country from Russia, she didn't need a fair housing bill to live anywhere she chose. The foreign exchange students who come to this country from Russia do not need fair housing bills to find lodging in racist college towns. Yet when they go back home, they will use their newly acquired knowledge to help their government kill American soldiers.

If I lost my life in Vietnam fighting for my country, the federal government would give my wife $10,000. Yet she could not take that same $10,000 and make a down payment on a house in any neighborhood of her own choosing. That is an insane injustice.

If my Daddy had been killed in World War II, this would be my twenty-sixth year of living without a father. Yet that same German who fired the gun to kill my Daddy could move to this country and buy a house in a neighborhood where my Daddy's son would be excluded. That is an insult. Is it any wonder that black people want to destroy *all* houses, block by block and brick by brick?

Black people in America know that white folks would be burning cities to the ground if they had suffered the same insults Negroes have suffered. We can see proof by their actions in Vietnam. If white folks will burn an entire country to free a foreigner, we know what they will do to free themselves.

Mental Slavery

It is strangely ironic that the American white man is not really free. He is the victim of his own insanity. The free man is the man with no fear. If a man fears my living in his neighborhood, eating in his restaurants, dating his daughter or going to his schools, he is my slave whether he wants to be or not. He is more my slave than my ancestors were his. When my forefathers broke that chain off their black ankles and fled to Canada, they were free. But when a man is enslaved in his own head, he can never be free. An American white man can go to Moscow, Russia, and see a Negro with a white lady and go crazy, because he takes his mental enslavement with him all over the world.

This country is indeed insane. America is gripped with a dangerous mental illness which is reminiscent of biblical prophecy. Jesus spoke of a time when fathers will deliver their children up to death and children will rise against parents. Present conditions in America are even worse. Never before in history has a foreign situation so pitted brother against brother and parent against child. Parents are siding with the government against their children over the issue of the Vietnam war. Yet their children are merely standing up for their moral rights. There is nothing wrong with an eighteen-year-old youth saying to his government, "If I am too young to vote, I am too young to die." A young man has the right of conscience to choose if and whom he will kill.

Yet parents support the right of the government to take their sons and send them to Vietnam to die. Suppose you hear a knock on your front door one morning. When you open the door you find an official of the federal government standing there who identifies himself properly. You ask him what he wants. And he answers: "Give me your household pet; your cat, dog or parakeet." You are naturally confused and you ask what he wants with your pet. And the government official informs you that the federal government needs the pet and there is no assurance it will not be killed. You would be outraged and you would resist such an insane and inhumane request. And your outrage would be supported by the Society for the Prevention of Cruelty to Animals.

Yet every day in this country the federal government sends a letter to American parents saying, in effect, "Give me your son and there is no assurance that he will not be killed." The parents of this nation have yet to raise a serious protest to this governmental practice. No one objects to the slaughter of a mother's child, but don't molest a household pet. Is it any wonder youth all over this country are protesting such insanity? The youth of this nation have a right to be outraged and parents must wake up to this reality.

Five or ten years ago, if Americans had picked up a newspaper and read that four Russian students had been arrested in Moscow for burning their national flag, everyone would have said, "Well, that's Communism for you." Today we have a law in this country prohibiting flag burning. America's insanity has reached such a point that people find it necessary to burn the flag.

Such a law is in itself insane. Think what a flag really is. It is only a piece of cloth, just as a draft card is a piece of cardboard. Personally I have no special respect for a piece of cloth. I am much more concerned about human lives. When we learn to salute one another in this country as brothers, with the same dignity and respect we show to the flag, brotherhood will become more than a pious phrase.

Youth Power

It is my hope that the youth of America will be the antidote to moral pollution and will bring this nation back to its senses. Those youth represent the greatest moral potential in the history of this country, perhaps,

even, the history of the world. It is possible for me to
check into a hotel one night and burn to death in my
sleep, if the hotel catches fire. But I would never walk
into a hotel which is on fire with the intention of going to
sleep.

The young people of America know that this country
is on fire and they have no intention of sleeping through
the moral revolution. I regret that when I was young, I
did not work as hard to clean the American moral atmosphere as many of today's youth are working to create a
better environment for my own children.

My first forty-day fast was to show my appreciation
for these American young people. It wasn't for myself.
Though I was protesting the war in Vietnam, I knew I
wouldn't be drafted. I am thirty-five years old and I have
six kids. And with my political beliefs if I *tried* to enlist,
the government would burn my draft card. I went forty
days without eating, drinking only distilled water, merely
to say "thanks" to these American young people and to
let myself suffer for not working as hard when I was
young as they are working now.

Many young people ask if they should join me on my
fasts.* I urge them not to. Politicians do not take the
youth protests seriously because they know these kids
cannot vote. But there are other things which they can do
to take direct action. I have personally vowed that I will
not shave, get a haircut, or wear anything but work
clothes until the war is over in Vietnam. And I urge all
youth to join me.

If enough young people go without a haircut, although
they do not vote, the barbers will make sure their protest
is heard. Or if enough kids go without shaving, some old
woman who doesn't give a damn about the war in Vietnam, but who just happens to have 15,000 shares of
Gillette Blue Blades, will voice the youth protest on their
behalf. If large numbers of kids refuse to buy any new

* Editor's Note: Candidate Gregory is currently on an extended
fast. He will take no solid foods until Election Day, 1968.

clothes until the war has ended, the garment industry will make sure it is over in a hurry.

Think of the federal tax money which is raised from the sale of cigarettes—money which is used to continue the slaughter, burning and maiming of innocent people. If youth all over America would decide to smoke their last cigarette and mail the empty pack back to the manufacturer with the message: "I will not smoke again until the war is over in Vietnam," the tobacco industry would kick the President's door in. If the tobacco industry is faced with the choice of "freeing the people in Vietnam" or going out of business, everyone knows which alternative they will choose.

I hope also the youth will remember, when they are planning their summer and deciding where they will go to help human suffering, that there is a poor white hillbilly in this country who is as poor as colored folks could ever be. I hope some of the youth will go into that white ghetto and let that white brother know that there is a better way of life for him too. Do not be fooled into thinking that all poor white folks live in Appalachia. Poor white folks live in every large urban area in America.

If conditions do not improve for these poor white folks in the next eighteen months, people will soon be calling them "rioters" and "looters" also. The only reason they have not been rioting so far is that this corrupt system has given them a Negro to play with. But there is a new black man in America who refuses to be used as a toy. Soon the poor white brother will feel the pain of insult, as Negroes have been insulted all their lives. And that insulted white man will be starting fires too.

I know my words sound very harsh, especially when compared to the compromising statements of other Presidential candidates. But please remember that politicians concern themselves with impressing the voter. They try to create an impressive image to win the vote. The statesman concerns himself only with telling the truth. Though

I do want your vote, I am not trying to *impress* you, only to *inform* you. When the election is over, whether I win or lose, you will be able to say honestly, "Brother Greg didn't lie to us."

It is true that I am very bitter and very angry. I do not hate America, but I despise the moral pollution which infects the national body. This is why I am running for the nation's highest office. I want to cleanse the moral atmosphere in America. America is my home and I do not plan to move anywhere else. I imagine I would be fighting just as hard to clean up my homeland if I was born and raised in Russia.

I have a dream and a vision of seeing the Constitution of the United States implemented in full for the first time in American history. It is a decent document on paper. And I want to see the Constitution function for the cause of human decency. After we have implemented the Constitution fully in this country, we all might decide to tear it up and start again. But I do not consider that option until I have seen what life under the full implementation of the Constitution has to offer.

CIVIL RIGHTS DEFENSE

Have you been reading in the paper how the United States keeps losing its nuclear bombs? Now how do we do that? I used to do a lot of silly things when I was a kid, but I don't remember losing any of my firecrackers . . . Now I don't want to wish any bad luck on my country, but if we must lose nuclear bombs, I hope the next one we lose will be in Harlem . . . and I find it . . . I'd take that bomb and put it on my shoulder and go down to Montgomery, Alabama, and march in front of George Wallace's house . . . singing, "We Done Overcome" . . . George Wallace would take one look at that bomb and come out and join me in the second chorus, "Y'all Done Done It, Baby" . . . Then I'd take that bomb and go to Washington, D. C., and walk right on the White House lawn . . . And I'd be sassy . . . I'd step in Lady Bird's tulips . . . and I'd stand under LBJ's window and yell: "Hey, is the Bird Man in? . . . Well, tell him to wipe all that barbecue sauce off his face and come down here . . . I want to talk to him . . ." I bet we'd get it all then.

ALL THE WAY . . .

LBJ really said he was going to declare war on crime in his State of the Union address. I'm all for it if he appoints someone over it who really understands crime . . . Like Bobby Baker.

But when I get to be President, I'll be fair. I'll have one white cat in my cabinet . . . And since LBJ gave us our first colored cabinet member, I'd make him my white cabinet member . . . I'll make LBJ Commissioner of Barbecued Ribs.

Have you noticed that everything seems to have gone wrong for LBJ since he visited the Pope? In fact his luck has been running so bad, I wouldn't be surprised if he asked for an audience with Elijah Muhammad.

Chapter IV

MORAL FALLOUT

It is traditional for Presidents to offer catchy phrases to describe their administration. America has been offered a Fair Deal and a Square Deal in the past and has seen the vision of a New Frontier and a Great Society. My administration will be the Clean Society. I will begin immediately to rid the national atmosphere of moral pollution and corruption in government.

To symbolize my intent, I will set aside a sum equal to one-half my Presidential salary to be offered as a reward for any information leading to my arrest and conviction for wrongdoing in office. I will also offer legislation saying that a sum of $10,000 will be put in escrow by the federal government for every Senator and Congressman elected to office. Again, that money will be offered as a reward for information leading to the arrest and conviction of *any* Senator or Congressman who is guilty of wrong-doing in office. I feel that the federal government has a responsibility to demonstrate its total opposition to corruption. It is a sad day in America when journalists and magazines have to offer under-the-table payoffs to office workers for information leading to the public exposure of elected officials.

The $5,350,000 set as reward money is a small sum indeed when compared to the billions wasted in other budget areas. Surely the federal government can set aside money equal to the profit from one good missile contract to demonstrate its integrity and credibility. I would hope that the $5 million would be a one-time budget appropriation and that it would be the safest money the government ever invested. I would hope and expect that the money would never be claimed because of the impeccable moral conduct of Senators and Congressmen during my administration.

America's Genocide

The fallout from moral pollution in this country has spread into every area of governmental operation. And an infected government spreads contagion to every other government it touches. Perhaps it is United States involvement in Vietnam which is responsible for the callous indifference to human life on the part of the Saigon government. For example, during the first twenty-six days of February, 1968, 5,488 civilians were killed and 9,395 were wounded in South Vietnam. And that does not include casualties in the Saigon area. Official government compensation to the families struck by such tragedy was $34 for a mother and $17 for a son or daughter. Human life is cheap to the South Vietnamese government, yet the United States pays the high price of approximately $500,000 for each Vietcong killed.

Stokely Carmichael and others have accused the United States of genocide in Vietnam. He was called a Communist and a traitor by the "good patriots" of this country. But I wonder if those same patriots know the story behind the cutoff of the United States' pharmaceutical supplies to Vietnam?

Vietnam has a complete assortment of the world's diseases—malaria, tuberculosis, cholera, typhoid, polio, intestinal diseases and parasites. A New York Times report of July, 1967, added bubonic plague to the list of diseases. The cruel, dirty and bloody war has added other infections and physical disorders. Since 1965, the United States has been supplying two-thirds of the pharmaceutical supply to Vietnam through AID (Agency for

International Development). In July, 1967, we stopped sending pharmaceutical supplies to Vietnam, in spite of the desperate need of Vietnamese civilians.

The reason we gave for stopping our shipments is that we couldn't control the corrupt American and Vietnamese businessmen. Not only were the shipments being pilfered on the docks of Saigon, but also foreign aid was sliced in half by American businessmen before it ever left this country. Price jack-ups, inventory frauds and deposits in Swiss bank accounts were depleting the American foreign-aid tax dollar unmercifully at a healthy profit to big business.

The one pharmaceutical exception to the shipping ban was contraceptives. Evidently that commodity fits well into AID's antilife bias which would deprive an underdeveloped people of life-saving drugs. Moral fallout in this country has so infected national policy that our government would rather deliver a whole nation over to the ravages of infectious disease than conduct a full-scale prosecution of corrupt American businessmen. Genocide is a good name for that brand of moral pollution.

Theft and corruption are not the only ways the taxpayers' foreign-aid dollar is wasted. Sloth and carelessness contribute to the wastage also. In March, 1968, it was reported that AID spent $100,000 to build a water terminal and hire a barge to supply fresh water to ships in Saigon harbor. A year after completion of the project, not a drop of water had been delivered because no one had asked Saigon authorities for permission to tie into the city water mains. As a result, seven ships had to leave Saigon without unloading and return to Manila to get fresh water.

Americans who are upset over the crime in the ghetto streets should walk those streets and see the crimes of the ghetto merchant. The Federal Trade Commission uncovered the disgraceful statistic that prices in ghetto area stores in Washington, D.C., are 265 percent higher than in suburban areas. A sample item which cost retailers

$115 was sold to middle-income people for $150 and to poor people in the ghetto area for $300, because they were buying on "easy credit" terms. The income of the average high-credit customer was $348 a month for a family of more than four. Such an income is well below the standard necessary to maintain a moderate standard of living. Cases were uncovered where large families were paying as much as a sixth of their monthly income for an appliance or for furniture. Six percent of the victims of such ghetto extortion were welfare recipients. Though the Federal Trade Commission has reported the figures, it has failed to take any positive action to stop unfair credit terms.

Tax Loopholes

White Americans are morally indignant over the large numbers of black people on relief. But they accept so easily the immorality of tax injustices in this country. The nation's richest Americans do not pay income tax because of tax loopholes. I know about tax loopholes since I am in a high income bracket. It is possible for me to take an entire night-club audience out for dinner and it won't cost me a quarter because I can write it off my income tax as publicity expense. Yet some poor white or black woman who needs to write off her baby's milk expense does not enjoy the same privilege.

The wealthiest families in this nation pay no income tax at all. The hardest hit are middle-income taxpayers, those in the $10,000-to-20,000 bracket. The higher up the income bracket a man climbs, the less tax he pays. Statistics for 1964 show that 19 millionaires paid no income tax at all. Another 463 people in the million-dollar bracket paid less than 30 percent, on the average, though their tax rate was supposed to be 70 percent. The most gaping crevice in the tax system in America is the 27½ percent oil depletion allowance. That economic crater allowed Atlantic Oil Company to collect a cool $410 million without paying a penny of taxes. Marathon Oil got by without paying any taxes for four years before finally coughing up 1.8 percent of its earnings. Standard Oil of New Jersey, which has a greater income than most members of the United Nations, paid only 0.6 percent of its staggering profit to Internal Revenue in 1962. And in 1966, Esso paid 6.3 percent of its $1.8 billion profit as taxes to Uncle Sam.

Moral fallout in this country seeps corrosively into the tax structure and forces the poor and middle-income citizens to pay the bill for a war which will take the lives of their sons. Yet the large corporations which profit financially from the death of American boys pay little or nothing to perpetuate their depraved resources. A nation which depends upon the continuance of death and killing for its economic life cannot survive.

After I am elected President, I will do everything in my power to bring a halt to such economic madness. An excess-profits tax will be *must* legislation. I will propose more fair and equitable distribution of taxes on personal income. The dominant theme of my tax structure will be this: those whom the system supports must in turn support the system; and those whom the system abuses will not have to pay for that abuse!

Not only does big business fail to pay its own way, but it receives contracts and grants from the government and is powerful enough to force the government's hand. Industrial monopolies manipulate both the government and the American people. For example, the Big Three of the auto industry—Ford, General Motors and Chrysler—did not submit bids on governmental cars during 1967. They imposed a boycott on the federal government because of their objection to being forced to disclose detailed facts concerning safety devices on their new cars. Had it not been for American Motors, the government literally would not have had any cars for critical or routine operations. The Big Three do not want to submit to such basic humanitarian requirements as tire safety standards. It is as though they were saying to the federal government, "And leave the killing to us."

All the while the auto industry was making demands of the government, demands which went against the best interests of the American driver, it was continuing to fatten its purse with government contracts. General Motors had defense contracts in 1967 totaling $625 million; Ford got $87.4 million; Chrysler $164.7 million. And that's not all. The Big Three got outright research gifts totaling $53,166,000 for General Motors, $2,989,000 for Chrysler and $5,099,000 for Ford. They can keep many of the patents developed from this research. What is it they say about biting the hand that feeds you?

Whom Can You Antitrust?

Moral fallout in America beclouds the fact that "crime in the streets" is quite inconsequential when compared to crime in the corporation. Property losses due to street crime amount to approximately $4 billion. It is a token sum when compared to the revenue garnered by giant corporation monopolies through their criminal violation of federal antitrust laws dating from the original 1890 Sherman Act. AT & T alone—with "only" 2 percent of the economy—is paying $400 million in extra taxes to the federal government and charging the public for it. AT & T is under no obligation to pay these taxes, but the government suffers from an obsession to collect them. Thus do AT & T and the government conspire against the pocketbook of the American people. The Bell Telephone Company, a legal and "regulated" monopoly, acquires its capital through excessive issuance of stock. This practice is costing the American people about $2 billion per year. If that dubious activity alone were stopped, long-distance telephone rates could be cut in half, local calls would be much cheaper, and America could go back to the nickel pay-phone call.

Of course, the Federal Communications Commission,

which is in charge of regulating the phone company, has the telephone interests and not the public at heart. Commission members normally graduate to the payroll of the Bell Telephone system. At recent antitrust hearings, Newton Minow, former chairman of the Federal Communications Commission, served as a lawyer for Bell Telephone.

The supreme irony is that persons caught cheating the phone company are guilty of a federal offense and can be fined $1,000 and sent to prison for five years. Tens of billions of dollars are pilfered from the American people each year as a result of antitrust violations. Yet not a single person is being jailed. White America is more concerned with grabbing black "juvenile delinquents" who have to steal a purse just to use the phone.

Not only does the government refuse to attack crime in the corporation, but it enthusiastically supports such criminal activity. America's quinine stockpile was placed in the hands of a private Dutch company before the Vietnam war reached its major intensity in 1965. The Dutch cartel now holds the world's main supply of quinine. From such a position of power, the cartel has jacked up quinine prices 800 percent.

The senior citizens of this country suffer most from such price increases. A major derivative of quinine, quinidine, is used to restore and maintain a normal heart rhythm in patients suffering from irregular heartbeat, or cardiac arrhythmia. For about a quarter of a million older persons in America, the ability to purchase quinidine for daily use is literally a matter of life and death. But the heartbeat of the nation does not throb with compassion for its elderly sufferers and the government continues to encourage the quinine monopoly.

World compassion is also denied by the quinine stockpile. Quinine is a crucial ingredient in the treatment of malaria. Malaria afflicts 300 million people the world over and 3 million die each year. We have almost completely wiped out malaria in this country. The greatest use of quinine in this country is in the soft-drink industry, and to some extent for cough remedies. During the month of January, 1966, one large soft-drink industry imported over a ton of quinine for use in tonic water. That amount of quinine would be sufficient to treat about 23,000 malaria cases. America's quinine stockpile is sufficient to supply this country's needs for the next four hundred years. If we wanted to, we could completely eliminate death from malaria the world over and still have enough quinine in stock to take care of our own needs for the next fifty or sixty years. This nation has no moral defense when it places a higher value upon mixes for drinks than it does upon human life.

The antitrust division of the Justice Department could bring a halt to large-corporation abuses. It has been obvious for years that Chevrolet should be split from General Motors. Chevy leads the way in price increases and dominates the auto market. Yet Justice Department lawyers cannot bring themselves to walk four blocks down Constitution Avenue, in Washington, D.C., to the Federal Court building to file the necessary papers.

Will the Real Crook Please Stand Up?

It is depraved and absurd for this nation to talk about crime in the streets and yet continually turn its back on other crimes. The national refusal to prosecute the wealthy and the privileged is a major contributing factor in causing lesser crimes in the streets. When syndicate leaders are given an honored place of respect and admiration in our society, we cannot expect young teenagers not to aspire to be criminals. When big business cheats its way to power and wealth with governmental approval, moral fallout infects the entire nation. When we wipe out the crime syndicate, we will go a long way toward eliminating crime in the streets.

To counteract such moral absurdities, I would bring the CIA home for a while. Let it cease the overthrow of governments for a few years. Let us see if the CIA can redirect its energies toward wiping out the crime syndicate in this country and whipping big business into line. I see no moral defense for our government telling Saigon to get rid of its corruption when we allow the existence in this country of the most corrupt crime syndicate in the world. Such is the atmosphere of dictatorship; for a large nation to tell a smaller nation to follow a standard of behavior which the large nation is unwilling to apply to itself.

Stiff legislation, imposing severe penalties, must be enacted to counteract the deadly infection of this moral fallout. Our nation is able to enact legislation prohibiting politicians, police departments and public officials from working in collusion. Why can we not do the same thing with organized crime? Any time more than five people gather together for the express purpose of committing crime, this meeting should be identified as a syndicate and should be subject to severe prosecution.

It is difficult to establish precisely the price tag of organized crime. A conservative estimate of syndicate gambling intake alone is $6-to-7 billion. The heroin branch of the narcotics traffic is $350 million a year. Add to this other types of narcotics trade, prostitution, policy, loan sharking and bootlegging and you will see that organized crime is easily a $10 billion a year business. Organized crime and big business are inextricably locked together in an unholy alliance. Profits from organized crime are invested in "legitimate" business operations and the private business sector of our society insidiously perpetrates illicit practices. More disturbing is to recognize that one good government contract granted to a huge corporation guilty of antitrust violation represents the same degree of illicit profit as one branch of the Mafia.

National health can never be restored until the real criminals of our society are identified and brought to the bar of justice. At the present moment there are concen-

tration camps in our country designed to detain those
who oppose the insane actions of our government and
fully equipped for immediate use. They are located at
Allenwood, Pennsylvania (just four hours by car from
New York City); Avon Park, Florida; El Reno, Okla-
homa; Wittenburg and Florence, Arizona; and Tule
Lake, California. Concentration camps in America stand
as a classic symbol of this nation's preoccupation with
detention of dissent rather than reform of current
practices.

The McCarran Act, which has been on the books since
1950, is still the law of the land. Title II, Section 100, of
the McCarran Act provides that under certain conditions, the President may, on his own judgment, proclaim
the existence of a "national internal security emergency"
throughout the land. He can do so if: there is a declaration of war by Congress; there is an "insurrection" within the United States; there is an "imminent invasion" of
the U.S. or any of its possessions. Upon doing so, the
President's political appointee, the Attorney General, is
required immediately to "apprehend and detain *any person* as to whom there is reasonable ground to believe that
such person *probably* will engage in, or *probably* will
conspire with others to engage in acts of espionage or
of sabotage." I want to point out that the emphases
are in the original wording of the Act itself.

I am serving notice now that my administration will
concern itself first and foremost with known criminals
and established illicit practices. I am less concerned with
those who might possibly conspire against our government than I am with those who are currently conspiring
to mutilate the soul of this nation. I will seek the repeal
of the McCarran Act to eliminate that tangible expression of national psychosis. I will keep the concentration
camps of course and open them as summer camps for
the kids. I will encourage people to request permits to
use the concentration camps for picnics and barbecues
on national holidays. If Hitler had used his concentra-

tion camps for Passover celebrations, six million Jews would be alive today.

Any President looking for acts of sabotage against the American people has many examples from which to choose. A recent medical journal, for example, called the birth control pill "the most dangerous drug ever introduced for us by the healthy." Bloodclotting disorders resulting from use of the pill are responsible for 180 deaths annually among American women. Yet the Food and Drug Administration has yet to be moved to action. The birth control pill enjoys diplomatic immunity because it is seen as an important solution to the problem of world overpopulation. The pill is also being pushed upon poor welfare recipients at home. It is not extreme to suggest that the distribution of an unsafe birth control pill at home and abroad is an act of conspiracy against humanity.

Even the television industry is an act of sabotage against the American people, not because of poor programing, but rather because of the deadly rays emitted from the TV set, especially color sets. For example, an examination of 90,000 General Electric color television sets found them to have the potential to leak excessive amounts of radiation. National standards dictate that radiation over 0.5 milliroentgens per hour constitutes a health hazard. Color sets were found to be emitting more than 12.5 milliroentgens per hour; maybe even more, since 12.5 was as high as the testing equipment would register. That is 25 times higher than the allowable limits of radiation. Excessive radiation can create genetic imbalance, as well as vitally affect the thyroid, lungs and bone marrow.

One of the most frightening potential conspiracies is the rapidly developing brain control research. Dr. Robert Heath, Tulane University, Dr. David Krech, University of California at Berkeley, and Dr. José Delgado, Yale University, are among those scientists who have brought this highly questionable practice near perfection. It is now possible, indeed it is currently being done, to implant electrodes in the heads of human beings and control them electronically to create emotions and influence patterns of behavior. About a dozen years ago, atomic physicist J. Robert Oppenheimer warned that scientists who work with the mind would face responsibilities greater than any carried by the men who fashioned the atomic bomb. Oppenheimer suggested that such research opens up the "most terrifying prospect of controlling what people do and how they think and how they behave and how they feel." That terror is upon us, though I doubt you have read anything about it before. Just as few readers will have known the location of America's concentration camps.

When such vital matters affecting the future and destiny, the health and sanity of the American people are enshrouded in silence, one must ask who are the *real* conspirators and saboteurs? I plan to head a nonconspiratorial administration and to expose to public view and evaluation the kinds of issues and moral questions I have merely suggested in this chapter.

The Original American

There is no *greater* moral issue facing this country, no better example of the totality of this nation's infection with moral pollution, than America's gross injustice to the Indian American. Speaking in Chicago, Illinois, during April, 1968, President Johnson spoke these words to a group assembled at a fund raising dinner: "I ask you, if there is anybody in this room tonight who would trade where you are for where you were when you discovered this land?"

Shouts of "No, no, no" swept through the audience and I could not help feeling that there must not have been any Indians in attendance that evening! When the President's ancestors "discovered" America, the Indians were occupying their own land, governing their own affairs and enjoying the natural endowments of an unspoiled environment.

Now the Indians have been reduced to a total population of about 600,000. The vast majority live on or near reservations and are dependent upon meager government handouts of services. The unemployment rate among Indians is near half, 50 percent of Indian school children drop out before completing high school and the average age of death of an Indian is 44 compared with 65 for all other Americans lumped together. White America continues to slowly exterminate our Indian Americans as surely and decisively as did the American cavalry a century ago. America's history has always been slanted against the Indian. When the American history book reports a battle won by the cavalry, it is called a great victory. When the Indians won a battle, it is called a massacre. The suicide rate on the Indian reservations is ghastly. Suicide is responsible for the high death rate among Indian teenagers, so hopeless is the future of these young men. Alcoholism and mental and physical deficiencies complete the spectrum of the dehumanized existence of the Indian.

Much of the current protest against the war in Vietnam focuses upon America's violation of the Geneva agreement. It must be admitted that neither America nor the Vietnamese signed that treaty. But America has many treaties with the Indians, involving land rights, hunting, fishing and timber rights, which are being violated every day. After I am elected President, I will demand a thorough review of *all* existing treaties with Indian Americans to ensure that such treaties are not only upheld but enforced. All treaties which are found to be subtly working against the best interests of the Indians should be scrapped. If the United States government will invest $30 billion annually in a treaty it did not sign, which is the approximate cost of the Vietnam war, how much more should she be willing to invest in upholding treaty *obligations* with the Indians?

My administration will begin *immediately* to establish a crash program to bring the Indian into the mainstream of American life. Such action is long overdue. Current government programs have been described as an effort to move from "paternalism" to "partnership" in dealing with Indian Americans. Neither term has any real meaning. What is needed in this country is a simple, open and honest recognition that Indians are Americans like any other group. Like any other minority in America, Indians need the full freedom and self-reliance to do for themselves, to carve their own destiny in a national environment which respects their rights and human dignity.

I will set up a commission immediately, not to deal with the Indians, but to go onto the reservation and to expose existing conditions to the American conscience. To symbolize the manifest injustice perpetrated upon the Indian American, I will issue an Executive Order saying that no Indian can be drafted until America begins to demonstrate concretely that this is the Indian's country too.

I will also establish a similar commission to encompass the needs of other groups—Puerto Ricans, Mexican-Americans and all other minorities who currently lack an organized and established voice. Many such groups now have no established representation comparable to the NAACP, CORE, or the Anti-Defamation League. My commission will be a Commission on Civil Order and it will concern itself with creating an ordered life in the American mainstream for all citizens. It will be made up of representation of *all* minorities. It will solicit complaints from minority groups and will ensure the same kind of thorough investigation of those complaints as the Internal Revenue Service conducts to get to the source of income tax questions.

Such a functioning Commission on Civil Order would

hopefully render the work of the Commission on Civil *Dis*orders unnecessary. When all Americans are given fair and equal opportunity for growth and development, the seeds of resentment and hostility will blossom forth in the full bloom of shared citizenship.

WHITE RACISM IS A RIOT!

When I first saw the report of the National Advisory Commission on Civil Disorders, I thought I was reading H. Rap Brown's State of the Union address.

It's a funny thing. The Kerner report said the riots were caused by "white racism" and the newspapers cried "Extraordinary." I called it the same thing, "white racism," and the newspapers cried "Extremist."

To be frank with you, I don't believe in riots. In fact I turned in the cat who sold me my favorite suit.

I was in Detroit during the riot and saw a cat running down the street with a couch on his back . . . I said, "Hey, baby, you're not one of them looters, are you?" . . . And he said, "Hell, no, man. I'm a psychiatrist on my way to make a house call."

Of course my cousin did all right during the riot in Detroit. He got forty-two television sets . . . But he's in jail now . . . He had nerve enough to mail in one of those ninety-day warranties.

But now that the Kerner report told us that riots aren't our fault, that they are caused by white racism, we're going to demand better services on the stuff we steal—like five-year warranties on appliances . . . free alterations on suits and dresses . . . and refunds for empty liquor bottles.

Of course, riots are nothing new. They're just the ghetto version of a Fire Sale.

I tried to stop the riot in Newark. I saw one of my black sisters break into a gunshop and get two pistols. I ran up to her and said, "Hey, baby, riots only hurt our cause." And she said, "Damn the cause. I just caught my husband with another woman and I'm going to blow his brains out."

Chapter V

THE GREGORY REPORT ON CIVIL DISORDERS

The recent report of the National Advisory Commission on Civil Disorders, commonly referred to as the Kerner report, has created such a stir across the nation and has become required reading in so many American homes that I feel compelled as a Presidential candidate to offer my own "ghetto's-eye" view as an alternative report.

Quite simply, what happened in city after city during the summer of 1967, and this year in response to the brutal slaying of Dr. Martin Luther King, Jr., was *revolt*, which will lead to *revolution*. Many people insist upon calling the disturbances in our cities "race riots." But that is not true. They are revolts. There is a difference between riot and revolt, between rioting and revolution. And once you understand the pattern of each, you will understand what really happened in our cities.

Race riots result in a loss of lives. Revolutions result in a destruction of property. Two decades ago, there was a flurry of race riots throughout the country and many lives were lost, though there was a minimal amount of property destruction. In the ghetto revolts which have become increasingly a part of the American scene since 1964, the loss of life has been minor when compared to the tremendous amount of property damage. When man hates man, the result is a riot, with blacks and whites killing one another. When man hates a system, the result is revolution and the destruction of property owned by, and representative of, that system. Those who are currently engaging in ghetto revolt are more concerned with striking back at and destroying the system than they are with killing white folks.

When a brother in the ghetto throws a brick through the window of an appliance store at eight o'clock at night, he is obviously not interested in killing the white store owner. He knows that the store is closed and that the white merchant lives ten miles out in the suburbs. But the light is on in the store window and he sees that television set representing what the system produces but does not share; what the system encourages a man to want but refuses to provide the job or the income to purchase. It is the *system* the man in the ghetto hates and it is the *system* he wants to destroy.

The Changing Attitude

What has happened in the ghettos of the North has been the result of an attitude that has been building up over a long period of time. The Negro came North in an effort to escape the deprivation, abuse and oppression of the South. He expected to find a better way of life. But when he got to the North, his hopes and dreams were shattered. He found himself worse off than before. He was more separated, more cut off, more segregated than he had been in the South.

In the South, the Negro had a white man who was honest with him. More important, every Negro had a white man he *knew*. In spite of the daily abuse he suffered in the South, every Negro had a white man to whom he could turn when he needed bail money or money to finance funeral expenses for a member of his family. In the North, Negroes have been so segregated and concentrated into a ghettoized existence that most of them did not even *know* a white man, let alone one to whom they could turn for help.

But the Negro in the North could not bring himself to admit that he had become a part of the very system he thought he was escaping. Consequently he lied, both to himself and the folks back home. He said everything was all right up North. He wrote home saying, "Don't worry, I'm doing all right." It was the only way he could keep from losing his manhood and some semblance of dignity.

And the northern Negro also lied to his offspring. He told his kids that things were better in Chicago than in Mississippi. The kids knew how bad things were in Chicago, but they had no way to compare their lives with life in Mississippi. The northern Negro kid could justify his life, bad as it was, because he thought he would be worse off down South. Occasionally, however, one of those northern black kids would go to visit his grandmother down South and he would begin to see through the lie because he had a ball in Mississippi.

Then the civil rights movement came along and forced the lie out into the open. The Negro in Alabama, Georgia and Mississippi began pushing for his rights and his northern black brother was cheering as he watched the news reports on television. When civil rights legislation began to be passed, the northern Negro was forced to admit his lie to himself and to his kids. He saw that all of the civil rights bills were really enacted for the South.

It was a bitter pill for the northern Negro to swallow as he saw the Justice Department literally taking the poor, illiterate southern Negro by the hand and registering him to vote. He was filled with shame and resentment because the northern Negro knew what the system had done to his *own* voting rights; how he had sold his vote to party precinct captains who threatened him with eviction from the housing projects if he didn't vote for the machine candidate. And the civil rights legislation didn't cover that northern injustice!

Mental and Physical Abuse

The northern Negro realized that in the South he had been abused by the white man physically; but in the North the white power structure abused him mentally. And the northern black man began to develop an attitude which reflected this recognition. When he saw his southern brother challenge the police openly in civil rights demonstrations, the northern Negro began to resent the police brutality which he had always accepted as a fact of life in the ghetto. Cops have been beating black heads in the ghettos of the North for a hundred years, but until the civil rights movement came along the cry "police brutality" was never raised.

There is a difference between the mental abuse of a system and the physical abuse of readily identifiable individuals. In the South the enemy was clear. He was the redneck, bigoted cracker who could be marched against and resisted. In the North, the enemy could not be easily identified because white racism was so deeply woven into the fabric of northern political, social and economic life. The southern Negro's enemy was a man and the northern Negro's enemy was a system.

The difference between the mental and the physical is represented by America's two most treasured documents: the Declaration of Independence and the United States Constitution. The Constitution is a physical document. It describes a physical entity, a definite form and structure of government, and it outlines the methods and procedures by which that government will function. The Declaration of Independence, on the other hand, is a mental document. It articulates the spirit of revolution and advocates the overthrow of oppressive forms of government.

The Constitution is a right-wing document which

respects a certain form of government and clearly shows the proper way of functioning *within* it. The Declaration of Independence is a left-wing document which speaks of the tyranny of certain governmental forms and appeals to the conscience of decent men to resist and destroy such tyranny. The Declaration of Independence begins by saying what government *should* be: "We hold these truths to be self-evident, that all men are created equal, that they are endowed by their Creator with certain unalienable Rights, that among these are Life, Liberty and the pursuit of Happiness. That to secure these rights, Governments are instituted among Men, deriving their just powers from the consent of the governed." But the Declaration of Independence goes on to insist that whenever *any* form of government is destructive of those ends and when rights and privileges are denied over long periods of time, it is a man's duty to destroy or abolish that government. "That whenever any Form of Government becomes destructive of these ends, it is the Right of the People to alter or to abolish it . . . . it is their right, it is their duty, to throw off such Government."

The Constitution has become the document of the southern Negro and the Declaration of Independence has become the document of the northern Negro. In the South, Negroes marched and demonstrated for their constitutional rights seeking to resist and defy physical abuse, singing "We Shall Overcome." In the ghettos of the North, Negroes are enacting the spirit of the Declaration of Independence, seeking to overthrow and destroy the abusive system with bricks and molotov cocktails, shouting, "Burn, baby, burn."

The New Black Man

Until the attitude of the northern ghetto dweller is understood, there is no hope for solving this nation's social problems. When the United States Supreme Court

passed its famous ruling on school desegregation in
1954, all black folks took a psychological cop-out. We
didn't really want to confront the white man, so we
unconsciously said to ourselves, "I won't realize the
benefits, but, thank God, life will be better for my
children." We took the Supreme Court decision at face
value and passed on the encouraging word to our kids.
A teenager in 1954 is in his twenties now, like Stokely
Carmichael and Rap Brown. He has lived for a decade
and a half with his dream deferred and he can accept
the vision of eventual betterment no longer. Today's
black youth are demanding what their parents unwit-
tingly taught them to expect.

The situation is further complicated by a shift in adult
attitudes. To understand the importance of that change
in attitude, you must know some things about the Negro
family which the Moynihan report failed to mention.
Negro youth have rarely been belligerent with the old
man. Black kids always listened to the old man in spite
of his ignorance. Even after we had been to college and
were too embarrassed to bring him out to meet our girl,
we still listened to Pop because old colored folks never
did take any abuse from the kids. You were always
"Junior" to the old man and he wouldn't think twice
about swinging on you. So you listened!

A decade ago, that old man was the one who was
talking about civil rights leaders expecting too much,
too fast; condemning the more militant actions and de-
fending the system. He was the voice of moderation and
passive acceptance of the status quo. But old folks aren't
talking that way anymore. The old man in the ghetto
has become bitter. He has seen the system pass him by.
He has seen the black militants getting all the poverty
money, all the good jobs and all the attention in the mass
media. He has seen white kids who were classmates of
his children holding down high-paying jobs while his
own kids are unemployed. That old man in the ghetto

is bitter now and he is the most dangerous Negro in the world.

If I was a white President and wanted to save this system, I would put every Negro over fifty under surveillance. His voice used to be one of calm and moderation and now it has become one of bitterness and frustration. That old Negro used to sit around whittling his stick and telling stories. He used to talk about baseball, giving his nitty-gritty philosophy and talking about the good white man he knew. He was beautiful; he was a philosopher and an orator. But he is bitter now and he is not telling stories any more. Along with the black youth, the old Negro has his "attitude."

There has been a change in attitude throughout the whole unique hierarchy of the Negro community. Traditionally the doctor has been the big man in the Negro neighborhood, occupying the top level of the black echelon. This is not true of the white community. The Rockefellers, the DuPonts, the Fords, the Kennedys do not send their children to medical school. So obviously the doctor is not the number one man in the white community. But he has always been in the Negro neighborhood. The hierarchy of the black community has been M.X the doctor, the preacher, the school teacher and the pullman porter. The pullman porter was a fascinating person to black kids because he did so much traveling. He was the man who would come back to his neighborhood and tell everyone first-hand what California was like.

The barber was also among the top echelon of the black community. Young people listened to the barber, regardless of how wrong he might have been. The barber was a respected businessman and even the militant spokesmen could not overshadow him. The school teacher had the captive ear of black youth and taught them that the way Ralph Bunche talked was the right way to speak. The teacher represented wisdom and taught American history from the white folks' book.

Traditionally, when we went to see the doctor, we found him talking about America the beautiful. When we went to the barber shop, we heard the same thing. And then along came Dr. Martin Luther King, Jr., and he took over the spotlight. Dr. King began to openly challenge the white power structure and consequently gained the admiration and respect of all black people. The doctor, the preacher and the barber found themselves being relegated to second place. Their talk of America the beautiful and their moderate defense of the system were no longer popular.

So what did they do? The doctor and the barber began to talk militant also, to try to recapture some of their lost prestige. In the doctor's office and in the barber chair, one could expect to hear, "White folks ain't no good." The doctor and the barber did not know why they were talking more militant, but it was to stay ahead of the Dr. Kings, the Stokely Carmichaels and others. Such talk instilled in the Negro something he had never heard before. He had never heard the doctor talking about rioting nor had he heard the barber talk about anything but football. And the talk began to spread to other persons who were trying to recapture their prestige in the Negro community—the pimp, the whore and the policy pusher. All joined in voicing a new black militant stance.

Consequently the Negro youth heard talk against white folks from people who had traditional status in the black community; people who were respected more than Mom and Dad. And the black kid believed what he heard that "white folks are no good" because he had heard the white boss call his parents "nigger." When he heard his feeling voiced and substantiated by the doctor and the barber, the black kid began to develop his own attitude; an attitude which was ripe to break out into riot.

The Cop and the Hunter

A new ghetto attitude developed toward the cop, although he didn't notice it. Respect for the northern cop has always been based on fear. But when the southern Negro began to march against Sheriff Jim Clark in Selma or Bull Connor in Birmingham in seemingly fearless confrontation, the northern Negro had to cast aside his fear of the cop also, or else face the humiliating admission that the southern black brother was braver than he was. This the northern Negro could never do. Whenever the northern cop began using too much force or shooting thoughtlessly, he was resisted by the brother in the ghetto. The cop did not understand the change in attitude of the northern Negro or the reasons for that change. All the cop knew was that he was being resisted for the first time, even though he was behaving as he always had.

The northern white cop brought into the ghetto the same psychological attitude the hunter brings into the forest. It is a violent sickness, an ego feeding device to prove one's manhood. The hunter goes into the forest with his rifle and when he fires it he experiences a feeling of power and his masculinity is affirmed. The act of shooting produces an exhilarating feeling and hunting becomes a thrill. But after the hunter kills his first deer, he is under an obligation each time he goes hunting. If he fails to make a kill, his manhood is denied.

The hunter goes into the forest, affirms his manhood and departs leaving behind a trail of suffering, violence and death. He sees the deer only as an object; as something to be used, manipulated and killed for his own purpose, to feed his own violent psychological sickness. If he spent some time living with the deer, the hunter would come to love the animal and could no longer kill. He might even be moved to want to shoot other hunters. But if the deer organized themselves and took away the hunter's gun, refusing to be fired upon, the hunter would be filled with resentment. He would be threatened because the means of his affirming his manhood would be involuntarily taken away.

The black man in the ghetto has been the white cop's deer. The white cop does not live in the ghetto nor does he really know its residents. Like the hunter, the white cop comes into the ghetto eight hours a day, does his "hunting" and then leaves. He affirms his manhood by beating ghetto heads. But when the man in the ghetto decides to affirm his own manhood and refuses to be misused, the cop resents the action and does not understand. All the cop understands is that a former mode of behavior has been suddenly taken away.

But if the cop had lived in the ghetto, he would have noticed the gradual change in attitude. He would have noticed that different look in the eye of the ghetto dweller. He would have seen a new pride in the gait of the man in the ghetto as he walked down the street.

Had the northern cop noticed the change in attitude, he might have conducted himself a little differently. The ghetto resident is very much aware that cops do not bother the pimp, the pusher and the whore. Such persons have always enjoyed free run of the ghetto. But the cop made the fatal mistake of picking on the black militant, the one who was trying to uplift the lives of ghetto residents. And the ghetto resented it. All at once the pimps who used to be heroes in the ghetto lost their status. Ghetto people used to look up to the pimp because he wore the forty-dollar shoes and the Beaver hat. He was Hollywood to the ghetto dweller; the closest the poor man could get to the consumer luxuries of society.

The new hero is the raggedy-dressed militant who is defying the system, talking loud and drawing a crowd. He is saying "Whitey ain't no good and all cops should be killed," and the ghetto is listening. It is listening because that outspoken militant is telling the truth about a corrupt and immoral nation. He is pointing out the national respect for violence. He tells of a nation where everyone knows who Al Capone and Jesse James were, but few citizens can name the great scientists and philosophers of this country. He tells of a nation where the Mafia is a household word but an appreciation of black heritage is nonexistent. And the ghetto knows he is telling the truth.

When the white system opens its eyes to the changing attitude in the ghetto, senses the growing mood of insistent militance, feels the pulse beat of ghetto resentment over the abuse of nonviolent people and the refusal to respond to the just demands of human need, it will begin to understand why riots happen.

Political Agitators and Ghetto Revolutionaries

Though the Kerner report placed the major burden of blame for rioting on white racism, I hold the politicians primarily responsible. Politicians are more to blame than the average white citizen because they have raised their hand and sworn an oath to uphold the Constitution of the United States. The Constitution gives a man the right to call me "nigger." That is freedom of speech. Freedom of expression under the Constitution gives a citizen the right to both hate me and verbalize that hatred. But no man has the constitutional right to place structural limitations upon my freedom. A man does not have to like me to work by my side, or in my employ or to be my next-door neighbor. But he does *not* have the right to limit my opportunities for employment or my choice of housing.

Politicians in this country have been more concerned with maintaining the positive public opinion of the white electorate than they have with upholding their oath to implement the Constitution. They are making a fatal mistake and must be held personally responsible for the continuation and spread of rioting. The temper of our time demands that political actions be determined by considering how they will affect black folks rather than white folks. It is black reaction which will determine national survival. White folks are not going to burn this country to the ground. The average white man cannot possibly be as bitter as the average black man. The white man has a better job and cannot afford to go to jail. He has much more to lose by participating in civil disobedience or open rebellion in the streets.

The ghetto brother whose anger and frustration has driven him to rebellion does not fear jail. He knows that life in the jail-house cannot be any worse than his present condition. In many ways it is better. The jail is warm, three meals a day are provided, and when the brother comes out of confinement, he is a hero back in his own neighborhood. In a very real sense he is regarded as a freedom fighter and he enjoys a dignity and respect never before accorded him in his life. It is the attitude and potential reaction of just such a man which should concern politicians.

It is this unknown man in the ghetto who is the real threat to national survival. He is strangely faceless, unknown both to the white power structure and to the militant black spokesmen. The government has become so preoccupied with the more vocal representatives of black militance—Rap Brown, Stokely Carmichael or Dick Gregory—that it has failed to see this invisible man in the ghetto. While the CIA is tapping the phones of the spokesmen and the national press is following them around, the man in the ghetto who will really be the backbone of the revolution slips by unnoticed.

The Detroit revolt was a good illustration. When Detroit first began to burn in 1967, every identifiable militant black spokesman in the country was in Newark, New Jersey, attending a conference on Black Power. If Detroit had been a premeditated matter, planned and perpetrated by Black Power leadership, the leaders would have been in the area guiding and directing the action. Instead they were hundreds of miles away talking about the future of Black Power. And America should realize that the very Black Power leaders it vilifies are the true patriots. They are openly articulating a warning to America of impending doom. They are giving a voice to that invisible ghetto presence which will one day act to make the warning a reality. America must heed the warning of her black patriots or suffer the consequences. Whatever the reaction, the nation cannot say it was taken by surprise.

The ghetto revolts up to the present moment have been the result of spontaneous reaction to a triggering incident—an open expression of police mistreatment usually or, more recently, outraged response to the assassination of Martin Luther King. Notice the pattern of ghetto revolt thus far. When the National Guard left the ghetto area, nobody else came in to fan the fires of revolution. If the current ghetto revolts were other than spontaneous outbreaks, that is, the work of outside Black Power agitators, such persons would have moved into action as soon as the Guardsmen left the area.

Those who are responsible for the triggering incidents are the real "outside agitators." And politicians who remain aloof from the needs of the ghetto must also share the blame for outside agitation. The failure to respond to the just demands of nonviolent leadership is an extremely agitating force.

But the climate is ripe for a shift from revolt to revolution. People who have been arrested and jailed in past ghetto revolts are beginning to come out of confinement. Many such persons were imprisoned for something they did not do. In their anger, cops swept whole street corners clean and grabbed the innocent with the guilty. These persons have been political prisoners and during their imprisonment they have developed an attitude.

Imagine a man who went out into the street during a ghetto uprising looking for his kids. He is a respected father and has a decent job. He found his kids cheering the street activity. And before he has a chance to get his kids back home, the cops arrest him along with the mob. The man is not really worried because he knows that he is innocent and expects to be released when the record is set straight. Then he finds a $50,000 bail placed upon him and hears false charges read against him. He faces an all-white jury which is more inclined to believe the testimony of the police than his own true story. He ends up with a year or two in jail and he knows his only crime was being black.

A political prisoner spends his time in jail seething with resentment. He is determined to get even with the unjust system which has confined him: This determination is the only thing which keeps him going while he is in jail. It is no accident that the great revolutionaries of history have all been political prisoners. A long period of confinement provides the opportunity to plan revolutionary action. The initial anger turns to shrewd calculation. The political prisoner develops a cool attitude, a more long-range view of the total struggle and a realization that change need not be immediate. He sees the futility of spontaneous outbreak and plans a determined strategy for revolutionary action.

I could almost predict who will be the leading revolutionaries in the ghetto by looking at the court records of past arrests and determining which persons have gone to jail for something they didn't do. Most Negroes arrested in past ghetto revolts have had a bad trial and many of those convicted have been innocent. When these political prisoners come back to their neighborhoods after they have been released, they are heroes and their time in jail is a badge of honor. Ghetto residents know the truth about false arrests. Thus, a political-prisoner-turned-revolutionary can easily amass an army of support in the ghetto. All those other ghetto Negroes who bear the stigma of false arrest are immediately sympathetic to the cause.

Calculated Revolution

But revolutionary action does not require an army of support. Spontaneous reaction involves larger numbers of people than calculated revolution. It takes only a half dozen committed men to bring a city to a standstill. Ten thousand black folks in the streets of the ghetto are like wind and snow; a momentary storm which runs its course in a few days. As always happens after a natural disaster, the National Guard comes in and cleans up the disaster area. But six skilled revolutionaries can control *G?* the destructive natural forces as scientists attempt to do with the weather. When the National Guard pulls into an area, the revolutionaries will pull out. And after the Guard leaves, they will move in again to initiate new action.

Calculated revolution uses the unique natural resources which nature provides to give power to the powerless. For example, it takes only one man to place dynamite in a New York City movie theater. Suppose that happens one day and the New York Times gets word that a Loew's theater will blow up in ten minutes. The dynamite is discovered in time to save the theater, but word is circulated that this action was merely one of many planned throughout the country. Do you suppose white folks will be going to the movies after that? Such calculated use of extremely limited resources could be powerful enough to bring the movie industry to a halt.

Or suppose one light-complexioned black revolutionary wanted to set off a spontaneous revolt but needed a triggering incident. All he would have to do is put on a policeman's uniform and go out into the street and beat up a little black kid. Then get in a car and pull away. Everyone would think it was a white cop, the triggering incident would be provided, and block after block would begin to burn. Such is the relative ease with which a disciplined and committed revolutionary can influence the national scene.

When shrewd calculation moves in to replace spontaneous reaction, white America cannot take comfort in relying upon "responsible" Negro leadership to stop revolutionary activity. There is an ethical principle involved. When the nonviolent marches were taking place and peaceful protesters marched singing "We Shall Overcome," the militant revolutionaries did not knock the picket signs out of their hands and replace them with guns. Even though they disagreed with the nonviolent strategy, the militants respected the right of freedom-loving people to demonstrate in their own way. Nor can the nonviolent leaders be expected to knock the machine guns from the hands of revolutionaries and replace them with picket signs. The same respect for a person's right to choose his own strategy of protest must be shown.

Rather than trying to silence the Rap Browns and the Stokely Carmichaels, white America should really be worrying about the day when the voice of warning is silent. Though white racism assumes that black people have a low degree of intelligence, we are not so stupid that we will stand on a soap box and tell you when we are actually going to burn the country to the ground. When the natural haircuts begin to disappear and everyone starts wearing conventional clothes once again, it will be a good indication that the real revolution is at hand. It is the man who blends in with the conventional American scene who is really able to strike by surprise.

Cancel the Flight

Civil disorder in America can be condensed in a simple illustration. Black people in America look at this country as they do a cigarette machine. They just can't communicate with it. Recall your feelings when you are running through the airport, just ready to board your plane, and you stop by the cigarette machine. You put your money in the machine, pull the lever, and no cigarettes fall down. Isn't that a frustrating feeling? Especially when you realize you <u>can't talk to the machine</u>.

Then you pull the change return lever and <u>you don't get your money back.</u> Suddenly you start doing little funny things with yourself. You tell yourself, "I didn't want Winston anyway, I wanted Viceroy.'" You pull the Viceroy lever and still no cigarettes. So you start pulling other levers. <u>Finally when you have pulled them all, you realize you are not going to get anything for the money you have invested</u>.

So you run over to the ticket counter and explain your problem. The man at the ticket counter says, "Look, I just write <u>tickets for TWA. I can't help y</u>ou. But there is a message written on the machine that tells you what to do." So you run back and read the message: "In case of problems with this machine, write to Giddings Jones, Kansas City, Missouri." Now you hear the last call for your flight and you stand there looking at that cigarette machine that you can't relate with and that has your money—<u>and your flight is leaving!</u> So you do the <u>normal</u> thing. <u>In a final act of desperation, you kick the machine hard. You don't get your money back</u> but <u>you see the dent in that machine and you feel better.</u>

But imagine your reaction if, after you had kicked the machine and turned away, a big foot came out and kicked you back. If that happened you would cancel your flight, take that machine and tear it up into little pieces, screw by screw.

Black people have invested their money, their lives, their labor, their faith and their trust in America for three hundred years. And we have received nothing for our investment. We took our problem to those who we thought would do something about it. We even went the long route and wrote to Kansas City in the form of nonviolent civil rights demonstrations. Still no refund.

So in the form of Watts, Newark and Detroit we kicked the American machine, trying desperately to get the attention of the nation. And in the form of the police, the National Guard, and even federal troops, the machine kicked back. Our desperation is now complete. We are saying to this country, "Cancel the flight." And we are going to dismantle this American machine piece by piece.

*The day of partial payment in
this country is drawing to a close.
For a hundred years America has
been changing the Negro's dollar for
thirty-two cents. Now she wants
to begin to make up for that injustice
by offering sixty-four cents.
We are out in the streets saying
to our country, "A full dollar's change
for a dollar spent. We are going
to stop this country from cheating or
the American cash register
will ring no more."*

—*Dick Gregory*

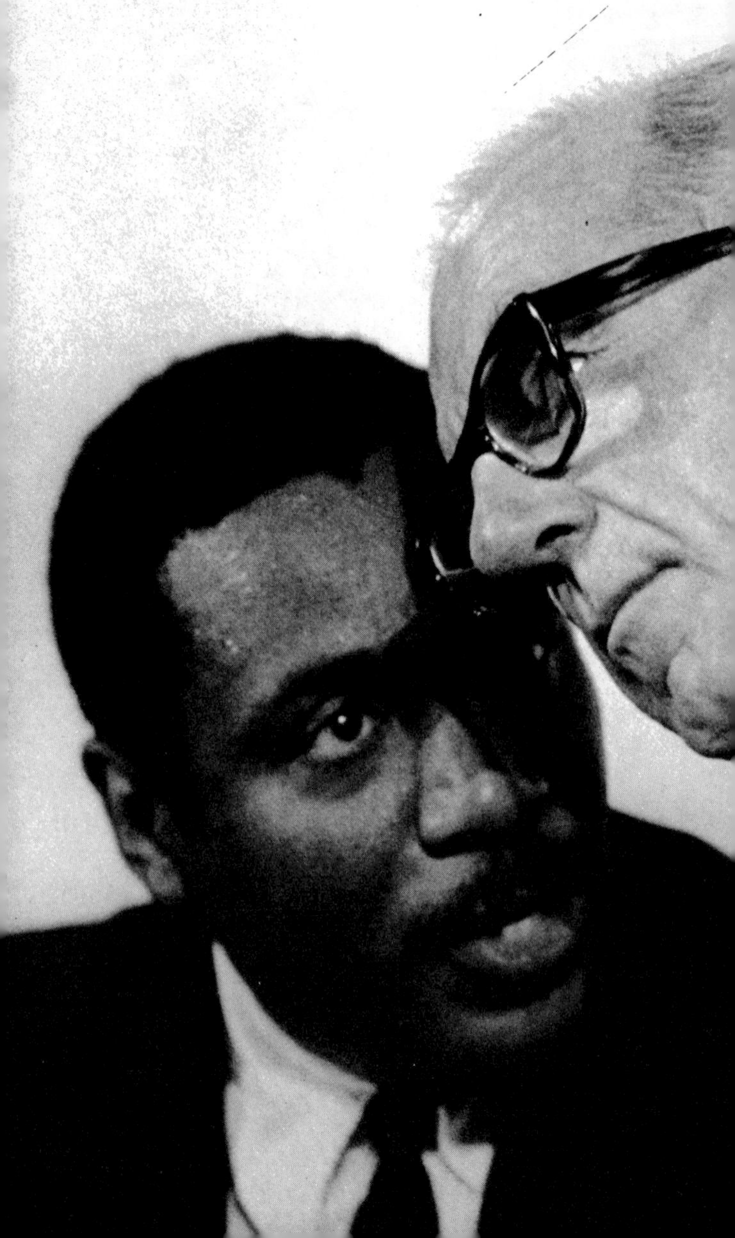

St. Louis FOR GREGORY IN 8

The Illustrations

THE CANDIDATE PROTESTS

I guess you know that I am not going to shave, get a haircut or buy new clothes until the war is over in Vietnam. I know it is dangerous. When I get to be President, the barbers might march on me with razors . . . singing, "We Shall Overcut."

Of course, I'd never burn my draft card. Out of respect for LBJ, I'd barbecue mine.

I'm not really worried about being drafted myself. I've got six kids. If you ever hear about me being drafted, you can believe those Red Chinese are marching in front of my house.

It seems like every time you pick up the paper it says something like, "400 Vietcong Killed—American Casualties Light"—which is really bugging the NAACP.

Of course, at the present time the Army isn't drafting married men with kids. Just the other day I saw a bunch of cats standing on the corner burning their wives' birth control pills.

But I'm getting sick and tired of some of the old folks in this country accusing our youngsters of being draft dodgers. Hell, we've always had draft dodgers. During the Second World War, if a cat didn't want to go into the service, he'd just slam a car door on his hand, or drop something on his foot . . . But what is making the old-timers mad is that these kids nowadays are beating the draft and they're not hurting themselves . . . They just go down to the draft board and claim they're homosexuals . . . Now prove that! . . . It's really something to see a cat go down to the draft board in a dress and say to the old recruiting sergeant, "Did you send for me, sweetie?" . . . And the old sergeant says, "We can't use you, but I can" . . . If this war in Vietnam has proved nothing else, it's proved that we've got a lot of young people who would rather switch than fight.

I would go to Vietnam only under one condition—that the government relaxes their narcotics laws. Those orientals have been smoking good "hemp" for two thousand years . . . And I'm not about to go over there and buck that hemp on some scotch and soda . . . They tell me they get so high that if you kill them they don't even realize they're dead . . . I heard a GI say he saw a Vietcong coming at him and the GI said: "Hey, baby, didn't I kill you last week?" . . . And the Vietcong was so high he said: "Yeah, man, I'm just bringing the bullet back."

Of course, if I was President there wouldn't be any of the young kids who would have to go to Vietnam. I'd go into all the prisons and draft all the sex maniacs . . . I'd give them some LSD and some tennis shoes and send them to Vietnam . . . I can just see the headlines now: "Twenty Vietcong Captured and Forty-seven Trees Attacked" . . . And when those plant lovers read those headlines, they'd make sure the war was ended in the morning.

WEIGHTY PROBLEMS

Of course, I am also fasting until after Election Day in protest against the war in Vietnam. This is my second major fast. Last time I went for forty days, from Thanksgiving until New Year's on nothing but distilled water. I started out weighing 158 pounds and ended up weighing 103. And believe me, I was weak. I was so weak I don't think I could have whipped Ronald Reagan's *former* staff . . . In fact, I've lost so much weight that nonviolence is no longer a tactic, it's a necessity.

And I'm so skinny now that when I go down South to demonstrate, they don't call me "nigger" anymore—they just call me "ger."

But I got some interesting hate mail during that first fast. I always get hate mail saying "You nigger this," and "You nigger that." But about the thirty-fifth day of my fast I received this letter: "Dear Mr. Gregory: This is to inform you that yesterday for dinner I had . . . fried chicken with gravy" . . . Now this was the first time I was aware that a colored cat somewhere hates me . . . We know white folks eat a lot of chicken, but we also know who eats it with gravy . . . "Mashed potatoes smothered with butter" . . . Well, that could be either white or black. But the next item really gave him away . . . "Black-eye peas with grilled onions." . . . Then he tried to throw it off and make me think he was white . . . "Jell-o topped with whipped cream" . . . "chilled Napoleon brandy" . . . Napoleon brandy and black-eye peas, there was a sick colored cat somewhere after he ate that meal!

My wife's cooking is so bad that the first week of my fast I *gained* ten pounds.

Chapter VI

THE GREGORY ACCORDS

The Conference takes note of the clauses in the agreement on the cessation of hostilities in Viet-Nam to the effect that no military base under the control of a foreign State may be established in the regrouping zones of the two parties . . .

— Final Declaration of the
Geneva Conference, July 21, 1954

The loss of all Vietnam . . . would have spelled the loss of valuable deposits of tin and prodigious supplies of rubber and rice.

— Dwight David Eisenhower*

Though this book is not intended to be a thoroughly definitive document on this nation's foreign and domestic policy, I want to indicate some of the major fallacies of current governmental approaches to problem-solving (*all* of which exemplify the actions of politicians) and offer the vision of a statesman and my dream for a truly human world order. No issue denies statesmanship as public policy more than America's current involvement in Vietnam.

It has been said that "power tends to corrupt and absolute power corrupts absolutely." Such corruption is absolutely true of America's policy in Vietnam. Through a strange reversal of the mandates of the United States Constitution, the President has assumed, indeed usurped, absolute power in foreign policy. The Constitutional De-

---

*Quoted from *Mandate for Change: 1953-1956*, Garden City, N. Y.: Doubleday & Company, Inc., 1963, p. 333.

bates at Philadelphia in 1787 clearly indicated that the
Senate, rather than the President, was to be predomi-
nant in determining foreign policy. The President is designated as commander-in-chief of the nation's military
forces and has the power of appointment for ambassa-
dors, councils and the like. Congress has the exclusive
power to declare war. The Senate is granted the power
to advise, consent and approve all foreign-policy commitments. The President has the power to initiate treaties
with other countries, for example, yet his commitment is
not binding without Senate approval. In all matters of
foreign policy, neither the President, the Secretary of
State nor any other official can commit this country without the agreement of the Senate. Yet today, our sacred
system of checks and balances has been illegally tipped
in the direction of the Executive Branch of the government.

An Executive Order

To counteract this Executive imbalance, I will issue
an Executive Order on Inauguration Day, January 21,
1969, establishing a National Council on Foreign Policy.
The new Council on Foreign Policy will have complete
jurisdiction over the use of American troops anywhere
in the world and will develop all American policy overseas. The dominant concern behind the creation of such
a council would be to willingly remove absolute foreign-
policy control from the hands of the President. My respect for and belief in the Constitution of the United
States demands that I seek to divest my office of such
awesome power; a corruptive power which embodies
the potential seed of dictatorship.

The National Council on Foreign Policy will be com-
posed of the following members:

1. The Chairman of the Senate Committee on Foreign Relations

2. The Majority Leader of the Senate
3. The Minority Leader of the Senate
4. One additional member from each party, elected by and from the Senate Committee on Foreign Relations
5. The Secretary of State
6. The President of the United States, serving as Chairman

As soon as possible after issuing the Executive Order, I will propose a constitutional amendment to Congress urging the establishment of such a National Council on Foreign Affairs on a permanent basis. Whether I am able to rally congressional support or not for my proposed amendment, my Executive Order will remain in effect throughout my entire term of office.

Policy determined by the National Council on Foreign Policy will be *completely* binding upon the President. The establishing of such a Council will pave the way for expressing a new degree of statesmanship in foreign-policy matters. Continuous planning and development will give a new role and image to America's participation overseas. The opportunity to exercise vision, rather than expedient self-interest, will be opened up. The new council will put an end to military dominance of foreign policy—a current state of affairs which is increasingly projecting America's image abroad as, to borrow Norman Mailer's phrase, "a bully with an Air Force." The absence of independent military dominance of foreign policy would go a long way toward eliminating the repetition of such embarrassing and alarming national fiascos as the Pueblo incident and the Gulf of Tonkin charade.

Those who would raise the question of separation of powers in the federal government must remember that the Senate already has an Executive function, rather than a solely Legislative function, under the current terms of the Constitution. Senate advice, approval and consent should inject it inextricably into the Executive role and should protect the American people from the ravages of dictatorial obsession.

Not only will I seek to restore and protect the Senate's role in determining foreign policy, but I will also propose legislation whereby the United States Supreme Court can rule immediately upon legal violations by the federal government. As a President and statesman committed to the best instincts of true democracy, I *demand* that my power and authority be shared with the Legislative and Judiciary branches of the federal government. And I will steadfastly resist all attempts to encourage me to do otherwise.

Justice and decency demand that there be a ready and available channel to the Supreme Court bench to force a ruling on military conscription and the legality of America's involvement in an armed conflict anywhere in the world. I will propose legislation to allow American taxpayers to bring suit against the federal government challenging the spending of a sizable portion of the national budget for a possibly illegal war. Young men who are drafted should be able to challenge the constitutionality of being required to serve in an illegal and unjust war. Those who have been imprisoned for refusal to cooperate with a draft system supporting illegality and injustice should be able to bring suit of habeas corpus for release from confinement and to encourage immediate ruling by the Supreme Court on the constitutionality of a particular war. The Supreme Court should have jurisdiction over *all* cases arising under the current conscription clause of the United States Constitution and should *immediately* be required to rule on any armed conflagration involving American troops which is not the result of a congressional declaration of war. Any time American troops are being used overseas as a result of orders by the commander-in-chief, the question of the constitutionality of such action should be immediately raised.

Law and Order—at Home and Abroad

There is no doubt in my mind that America is in Vietnam illegally. It is tragically ironic that the same people who demand law and order on our city streets are the most ardent supporters of America's denial of law and order in Vietnam. A nation which claims to be built on a foundation of law must also honor law abroad. An illegal introduction of American troops in Vietnam, an open and flagrant violation of the law, justifies armed revolution by those who seek a return to law, order and justice.

A memorandum to the President issued by the "Lawyers Committee on American Policy Toward Vietnam" clearly establishes the illegality of the American presence in Vietnam. United States actions in Vietnam violate the essential provisions of the United Nations Charter, to which this country is bound by treaty; violate the provisions of the Geneva Accords, which we pledged to observe (though we did not sign the treaty); and violate our own Constitution by prosecuting a war without an official declaration of war by Congress.

The State Department argues that our government's action in Vietnam is justified under Article 51 of the United Nations Charter sanctioning "individual or collective self-defense if an armed attack occurs against a member of the United Nations." Yet South Vietnam is emphatically *not* a member of the United Nations and, according to the 1954 Geneva Accords, is merely a temporary zone. Since those same Geneva Accords recognize all of Vietnam as a single state, the conflict there is a "civil war" and foreign intervention is forbidden. Our own President Abraham Lincoln vigorously resisted British and French threats to intervene on behalf of the Confederacy during this country's Civil War. Yet we turn right around, one hundred years later, and choose sides in the civil conflict of a tiny nation in Southeast

Asia. Certainly the British had more justification for intervention in America's Civil War, rationalizing such action as recovery of lost property.

Article 51 also speaks of the right of collective self-
defense. Nations which history and geography have
grouped together, which share a regional community,
have the right to gather together for collective self-defense. The United States does not qualify to participate
as a member of a regional collective defense system for
Southeast Asia. America is separated by oceans and
thousands of miles from Southeast Asia and we have no
historical or ethnic ties with the people of that area. The
suggestion that we are related to the people of South
Vietnam on any other basis than our own self-interest
is absurd. Former President Dwight Eisenhower gives a
clue to our real concerns in South Vietnam in the quota-
tion which heads this chapter.

The State Department has also contended that the
actions of the United States, "being defensive in charac-
ter and designed to resist armed aggression, are wholly
consistent with the purposes and principles of the [United
Nations] charter and specifically article 2, paragraph 4."
Yet that section states in clear and unambiguous lan-
guage that "all members [of the United Nations] shall
refrain in their international relations from the threat or
use of force against the territorial integrity or political
independence of any state or in any other manner inconsistent with the purposes of the United Nations." Such a
statement does not allow a nation such as ours to show
territorial favoritism in a legally divided country nor does
it say that "political independence" must automatically
be assumed to mean a democratic form of government.

The State Department has also justified our government's actions in Vietnam on the grounds that "the
North Vietnamese have repeatedly violated the 1954
Geneva Accords." Yet our government's repeated violation is seemingly not important. On July 21, 1954, Under Secretary of State Walter Bedell Smith, in a declara-

tion confirmed by President Eisenhower, pledged that our government would not "disturb" the Geneva Accords and would "not join in an arrangement which would hinder" the rights of peoples "to determine their own future." Yet we backed the Diem regime when it announced on July 16, 1955, that it would defy the provision of the Accords calling for national elections. The guarantee of free elections was the central provision of the Accords that made them acceptable to the Vietminh.

In addition, the United States chose to ignore the ban on the introduction of troops, military personnel, arms and munitions and the prohibition against establishing new military bases in Vietnam territory. The reign of terror under the Diem regime and its refusal to hold national elections caused the civil war in Vietnam in the first place.

Of course, most disgraceful of all is our violation of our own law and order; that represented by the United States Constitution. The Constitutional Debates of 1787 clearly indicate that the President shall have the power and authority to repel sudden attack, but war-making shall be the prerogative of Congress, through an official act of a declaration of war. Congress has *exclusive* power to declare war. This power is indisputably *not* granted to the President. This point cannot be emphasized too strongly. The President's call for more and more troops to be sent to Vietnam is the clearest possible violation of the Constitution of the United States. A President with so little respect for law and order can never expect domestic tranquillity and a cessation of crime in the streets.

Pulling Out

After I become President, I will insist that this nation display a respect for international law and order. I will refuse to break the law myself and since I am not supported by a declaration of war issued by Congress, I must immediately cease the hostilities in Vietnam. I must stop the bombing. I must recognize the territorial and political realities in that country and recognize the National Liberation Front. This I will do as a first step to sitting down in humble and honest negotiation.

I am realistic enough to recognize certain qualities, characteristics and emotions all men share, regardless of varying ethnic backgrounds. If I, Dick Gregory, was known to be the leader of a mob which was conducting daily attacks upon your home and family, would you sit down at the dinner table with me and talk about cultural exchanges and what we could do together? Of course not. Until I cease molesting your family, you will not trust anything I say to you.

In like manner, I realize that the North Vietnamese cannot possibly trust this country until we have eliminated the last vestige of molesting the Vietnamese family. Once this has been accomplished, I will talk personally with Ho Chi Minh.

I personally feel that Ho Chi Minh and myself will be able to converse together as statesmen. And I realize that the burden of sincerity will rest on my shoulders. I will begin by apologizing for the suffering inflicted on both sides of this tragic conflict. I will share my conviction with Ho Chi Minh that violence is a disease and that we have both been victims of a plague.

I will admit bewilderment concerning how this nation became involved in this terrible plague. The depraved disease of violence has its mythic depths in the Old Testament story of Cain and Abel. And it reached its most awesome proportions in America's inhumane leveling of Hiroshima. Like cancer, the disease of violence grows and spreads mercilessly. America entered this conflict with an aspirin tablet, seeing Vietnam as a small headache in world affairs. But as time wore on, we began to reach for a more and more powerful antidote.

Western science has come to understand that pain and

debilitation in the body are symptomatic of a deeper mental and physical disability. To arrest pain and yet fail to consider the deeper dimensions of illness accomplishes nothing and leads to death.

The seemingly endless hostility in Vietnam should have taught us by now that war is an unworthy instrument for settling disputes between nations. During my conversation with Ho Chi Minh, I will suggest that one of the tragic by-products of this terrible conflict is that we have come to know one another better and to understand ourselves more fully. America's dwindling prestige the world over has taught us that though this world respects power and violence there are certain limits of righteousness and justice which cannot be exceeded. And Vietnam has learned that the powers of evil can indeed be resisted, in spite of overwhelming odds.

So I will admit our national immorality and offer to start afresh on a new moral plane. If history judges such an action naive, so be it. I would rather accept the consequence of expressing my nonviolent naivete than face the terrible judgment of continued reliance upon violence.

My offer to Ho Chi Minh will be to replace violence with kindness. I will seek to conduct a massive program of rebuilding and rehabilitation to help undo the terrible destruction caused by our violent sickness. I will seek to build where we have formerly sought to destroy.

Honest negotiation with North Vietnam must recognize and understand a natural reluctance to trust any display of good faith from our government. I will seek to reassure Ho Chi Minh by working out a program of rehabilitation for Vietnam through the auspices of the United Nations. Funds for rehabilitation—relocation of displaced families, the rebuilding of cities, bridges, factories and so on—at least equivalent to the billions we have spent to destroy Vietnam would be offered to a United Nations Task Force designed to implement humanitarian concern. I will state clearly and unequivocally that the United States stands ready to rectify its past reign of terror *whenever* Vietnam feels that American aid can be accepted in good faith.

It has been said: "To err is human, to forgive, divine." The errors we have made in Vietnam fall into the category of the *inhuman;* and we have little right to expect forgiveness. We can only hope that the best instincts of humanity will prevail; that sincere repentance will be finally met with trusting acceptance.

The United Nations

As President of the United States, I will seek to exercise my influence to create renewed respect for the United Nations. Current lack of respect for the United Nations in some parts of the world is due to the domination of the UN by Russia and America. But the UN should be freed of domination by *any* nation so that it can really become a neutral moral force for human betterment. When two nations are engaged in conflict, wreaking their hostilities upon one another, the United Nations should truly be the unbiased, neutral moral force which paves the way for negotiation. This can only happen when the United Nations is clearly seen not to represent the special interests of *any* particular nation and is viewed as a true advocate for humanity.

I will urge a redistribution of power in the UN so that every nation has an equal voice in policy determination. Population, wealth or military power should give no nation an advantage over another when it comes to deciding what is best for the human family. Nations who choose not to join the United Nations should nonetheless be allowed to send observers. Under the current UN structure, observers can only come to sessions when a special invitation has been extended. Such exclusion of members of the human family is inexcusable for an organization designed for and dedicated to the promotion of world understanding and cooperation.

In addition to the United Nations headquarters in New York City, I will advocate the building of other UN buildings in four areas of the world. Every three months the United Nations General Assembly should meet at one of the four other locations to give the people of the surrounding area a feeling of sharing in world deliberation. Not only would such rotation of sessions promote better understanding of the work of the UN among peoples the world over, but it would expose UN delegates to different areas of the world and would acquaint them with the peculiar needs of particular peoples.

A total commitment to the eradication of human misery, the defeat of disease and the feeding of starvation should be the theme of the United Nations program. United Nations hospitals should be constructed in the remote areas of the earth where research on rare diseases is relentlessly undertaken and where poor suffering victims of such diseases are received and treated.

A United Nations Food and Health Fleet should drop anchor in international waters off the shore of most needy nations, providing medical supplies and treatment and distributing food. Such a fleet steaming into harbor flying the United Nations flag would be a magnificent display of hope to the two-thirds of the world population who are literally starving to death.

A United Nations Flying Squad could service the world in the interests of humanity. Helicopters bearing food, medical supplies, farming equipment, doctors, technicians could fly over the remote areas of the world dropping a well equipped nonviolent army of determined combatants who would wage a righteous war upon the ravages of human misery. A Farm and Conservation Department of the United Nations, utilizing the resources of the Flying Squad, could not only supply seed and fertilizer but also agricultural specialists to assist in planting crops.

The United Nations flag could become the banner of hope for the entire world. It should be flown everywhere; everywhere hunger, disease, ignorance and illiteracy crush the divine potential of human beings. The UN flag should become as prominent as Coca-Cola signs are throughout the world, reminding all men everywhere that nations, colors, religions and political orientations place no restriction upon membership in the human family.

Foreign Aid

If America would one day become as concerned over injustice as it is over Communism, we could eliminate unjust practices. It is the same with hunger, starvation, disease and ignorance the world over. When we become as afraid of these things as we are of Communism, that day we will show true human compassion and use our vast resources for the benefit of humanity.

America currently spends about $900 million in supplying United States arms to underdeveloped nations. This figure represents a doubling of the arms flow over a six-year period. The United States has 161 major military bases outside the country, and when minor installations are considered the figure soars to 2,200. This country is obsessed with military spending in the national budget. Military contracts are abused more than any other kind by large corporations, thus foreign-aid spending becomes a convenient racket for big business. The depth of fraud by big business in handling the foreign-aid dollar tempts one to seek to eliminate foreign aid altogether.

Yet in the interests of brotherhood and humanity we must always have foreign aid. We must make sure, however, that it is truly a sharing of our national resources and that it is designed to meet real needs of people in foreign lands rather than to project upon them our own military obsession. There are desperate needs the world over. In less than thirty years the world's present population (3.3 billion) will about double. Over four-fifths of this population explosion will take place in the poor nations. Even now, food production fails to keep pace with growing population in these areas.

About one-fourth of the world's land *could* be cultivated if money and training were made available. This land just is not used today. If it were, the world's food production would multiply four times. Even if the 10 percent of the world's land that *is* used for agriculture were *fully* utilized, ten times the present world population might be fed.

The basic ingredients of fertilizer—nitrogen, phosphoric acid, potassium and lime—can be produced in virtually unlimited quantities both now and in the future. Yet the production of fertilizer is of little value if the finished product is not placed in the hands of someone who knows how to use it. One of the current frauds of America's foreign-aid activity is that we supply fertilizer and agricultural supplies, yet fail to provide skilled technicians to assist the cultivation of crops.

Of course, the United States does not stand alone in being obsessed with military spending. In 1965, the world spent about $180 billion on armaments. Many experts believe that *one-thirtieth* of this sum would break the back of world illiteracy.

America must re-evaluate what is meant by developing "stronger" nations. A nation which is well equipped militarily, yet plagued with disease, hunger and ignorance, is not really strong. Moral fortitude has a unique strength all its own. As President of the United States, I would urge that 98 percent of all foreign-aid money be expended for health, education, food production and technical advance. I would seek to build stronger nations in terms of increased life expectancy, decreased illiteracy and the complete elimination of malnutrition, instead of focusing primarily upon military strength.

Such a shift in foreign-aid spending would change

America's image abroad. America would be known, not as the world's richest country, but rather as the world's most *humane* country. A true sharing of our vast resources will encourage people the world over to like us not as Americans but as *people*. When that happens, national boundaries and political differences become insignificant. America's preoccupation with sharing her resources must become so evident that people the world over will know that if American resources are not flowing into their nation, it is because their own leaders refuse to accept them. And even rejection by those nations which disagree with us politically should not discourage America in her determined effort to serve humanity. We must work with and through the United Nations to provide a neutral and nonpolitical channel funneling aid to people in need. Every villager in the most remote area on the face of the earth must come to know of America's concern for humanity. Let America stop delivering arms and start delivering food. Let America wage war upon the infant mortality rate the world over instead of encouraging preparation for war through the delivery of guns and tanks. Let America provide skilled medical personnel in the most remote areas of the world, devoting knowledge and research toward the elimination of rare diseases unknown on the North American continent.

An enlightened restructuring of America's approach to foreign aid could not only go a long way toward eliminating human misery the world over but could also solve domestic problems. In many areas of the rural South, vast numbers of unemployed persons constitute a huge potential work force. Currently there is no work for them and their relief status constitutes a drain on the system simply because that same system cannot provide employment. About a million farmers have sold their farms and moved into town since 1960 because of government control of crops. Volume of production has become so important that these farmers sum up the current farm situation in this country with the phrase "Either get big—or get out." The family farm is disappearing and being replaced by the large corporation-owned farm.

There is an obvious need for the government to go into such rural areas and develop industry. Suppose such action were related to foreign-aid concerns. The federal government could provide employment for the potential rural work force through the development of Foreign Aid Factories. The industry of a particular area in this country would be related to the needs of a particular country abroad. Suppose, for example, it was determined that Peru's greatest need was tractors. A Foreign Aid Factory could be developed in a depressed rural area of Alabama which would manufacture tractors for Peru. Money appropriated for foreign aid to Peru would be invested in the Alabama industry. It would go for payroll, building construction, the purchase of machines, vocational training and the like. Foreign-aid money would never leave the United States; only goods and services would be exported. Basic human needs at home and abroad would thus be served and the possibility of big corporation theft of foreign-aid dollars would be eliminated. There would be no extra cost to the federal government; merely a creative use of dollars appropriated.

In fact, both the local state and the federal government would benefit from such a use of foreign-aid money. Foreign-aid dollars used to employ persons in Foreign Aid Factories would, of course, be subject to state and federal taxes. Working people would be getting the money directly and state revenue would be collected indirectly. Additional financial savings would be represented by the decreasing welfare rolls, once more and more people are employed.

The small farmer would have additional options to selling out and moving to the city. He could participate in a vocational training program leading to employment in a Foreign Aid Factory. Or his farmland could be designated as "foreign-aid territory" and he would grow crops to be sent to feed people abroad. Farmland could be assigned to particular countries abroad, following the same pattern as the Foreign Aid Factories. Groups of farms would be growing food to feed particular areas of undernourished people.

Unless human compassion replaces military obsession as the dominant theme of this nation's foreign policy, America is doomed. Speaking of the greatness of Egypt in the early days of human history, Paul Christian said: "By means of settlement in Greece and Asia, Egypt promoted civilization. The great lawgivers and philosophers of antiquity all admitted that they went to Egypt to learn wisdom. Peace, that majestic quality of all great states, was held in honor there, because peace, the companion of justice, is also the nurse of genius. When Egypt had her first war-like pharaoh, in the 19th dynasty, she said goodbye to the traditions that had laid the foundations of her greatness. When she conscripted soldiers for ends other than those of defense, she taught her neighbors to measure her strengths and to estimate the extent of her armaments.

"At first Egypt owed her great victories, taking her even to the Ganges, to the fame which preceded her. Conquering races who fight without being drawn to war by any necessity in their nature only teach other races how to conquer them. Sooner or later they fall, conquered in their turn with their trophies among the ruins that they tried to build up again. That will always be what human glory comes to.

"The glory that was Egypt was to disappear under the heel of the Persians; as the Persians, in their turn, disappeared before the Greeks; who then themselves fell to Rome. And Rome finally fell to the barbarian hordes bringing a new world with them on the waves of their irresistible ocean."

The torrents of demand for world justice flood the American conscience. America will either become the ship of hope for all humanity or drown in her own selfish preoccupation.

THE GOLD DRAIN

I guess we all know there is a gold crisis in our country. Of course, I knew our money was in trouble before anybody else. A couple of months ago I saw some Indians standing on the corner trying to sell some dollar bills for old beads.

And last week my cousin had a gold filling put in his tooth. He looked at it yesterday and it's the brightest green you ever saw.

I understand the gold crisis is so bad, a group of dentists plan to march on the White House singing, "We wonder where the yellow went."

I understand they are really taking advantage of our gold troubles in France. They say De Gaulle just bought a twenty-four-karat frame for his mirror.

People used to call De Gaulle an extremist and all kinds of other nasty names. Nowadays they are calling him "Golden Boy."

But they tell me they are hoarding the gold so fast in France that even Old Gold cigarettes went up thirty-five cents a pack.

And I'm really worried about the gold in Fort Knox. I don't mean to scare you or anything, but I don't believe it's there . . . Like there's over 200 million Americans and I haven't and you haven't met anyone who has seen that gold . . . And I'm not taking anybody's word for it . . . I believe if the gold was really there, we could take "In God We Trust" off the money . . . That's what we ought to demonstrate about. We ought to all get together—black and white—and go to Johnson City, Texas, and lay in LBJ's barbecue pit . . . And when he sticks his head out the window and says: "What y'all want?" we'll say: "Show us the gold, baby!" . . . Because you can believe one thing. If there's any gold left, LBJ knows where it is . . . A lot of folks think LBJ is broke, but that's not true . . . A few years ago when they sent up that Communications Satellite, the minute they named it Early Bird, I knew it belonged to LBJ.

Chapter VII

LIFE IN THESE UNITED STATES

The report of the National Advisory Commission on Civil Disorders has paved the way for a real moral and political cleansing of the atmosphere in America. With the proper exposure, it could make possible an honest conversation between Americans, and the establishment of a social system of shared power, wealth and opportunity. Every effort should now be made to keep the Kerner report before the nation. An all-out campaign should be launched to sell the popularity of implementing the recommendations of the report.

When businessmen get together and decide they are going to sell the nation on using Oxydol, they buy prime-time national television advertising; they sponsor the most popular entertainers they can find; and they make every effort to saturate the national mind with Oxydol. The Kerner report should be made into a documentary. The government should purchase prime-time national television and saturate the nation's mentality with the findings of that report.

The entire volume should be made into a phonograph album. Youngsters in school should be encouraged to read and study the report. National and regional contests for school children, patterned after spelling bees, should be structured around knowledge of the Kerner report. Foundations, industry and other members of the private sector should be encouraged to give college scholarships to the winners of those contests. Parents will thus be motivated to make sure their children are reading and memorizing the Kerner report pages.

Disc jockeys and radio telephone quiz programs should be encouraged to call listeners with questions based on the report. The government should encourage civic groups, churches and private clubs to hold study groups and discussions. Conversations at cocktail parties, across bars and lunch counters, on airplanes, buses and trains, wherever people congregate, should throb with Kerner report one-upmanship. It should be a mark of pride for an American citizen to be the best informed Kerner report expert in his block.

A new base for national unity and understanding would result. Northerners, recognizing the depth of their own involvement in America's racial problem, would be forced to apologize to the Southerner for making him bear the brunt of racism for so many years. Northerners and Southerners, blacks and whites could begin to speak of an American problem rather than a racial problem. An honest admission of American racism would replace preoccupation with America's racial problem. And all minorities in this nation would profit from such an admission. For the first time all Americans would recognize racism as an American problem—not a Mississippi, Georgia, Chicago or New York problem.

Such a recognition could lead to a concern with implementing the United States Constitution rather than appealing to love and understanding. This nation has always believed in a separation between Church and State. I find it hard to understand why the Bible is always thrown at black folks when we really need the Constitution. The Constitution has a much more realistic attitude about love than does the Bible. If a man doesn't love his wife, the Constitution gives him the right to divorce her. But some churches say a man cannot get a divorce, which seems to make love irrelevant as a basis for marriage. So the Constitution is much more representative of basic freedoms than the Bible.

I am longing to see the day in this country when we will be as concerned about citizens as we are about dollars. Our government will go to any extreme to enforce income tax payment. Income tax laws in this country are enforced so rigidly that if a man violates them, he lives in constant fear of being caught. It would be a glorious day in America if civil rights were so respected that if a man violated them, he too would live in constant fear of being caught. When the civil rights of *all* citizens are so respected there is a good chance we will see the end of riots.

After I am elected President I will institute a national campaign of citizen respect. I would begin by reinstituting the use of the title Citizen. In the early days of American history, the title was widely used. People were referred to by their title of Citizen—such as Citizen Tom Paine. I would encourage Americans to once again begin calling one another by the title Citizen. I would have the title put on birth certificates, driver's licenses, marriage licenses and all official documents. Let Americans be known to one another simply as Citizens— Citizen Gregory or Citizen McCarthy. School children would begin early to use the title in the classroom. National Citizens Day would be a giant love-in when every Citizen in the country made a special effort to greet every other Citizen he met.

Citizenship is a feeling as well as a right. Once I feel that I am a Citizen I know that I am a full-fledged human being. Color, class and ethnic distinctions are irrelevant. They are all subsumed under the title Citizen. There is something terribly divisive in the way we have broken down the designation "American" into Irish-American, Italian-American, Spanish-American, Polish-American and so on. A return to the use of the title Citizen will undo such division.

Once we have come to recognize each other as Citizens at home, perhaps we Americans will see our role as world citizens more clearly. As President, I will also conduct a national campaign for World Citizenship. I will encourage all my fellow American citizens to be concerned with feeding their fellow citizens of the world. Meters will be placed in the parking areas of all federal buildings. Money deposited will be used to buy food for starving nations. Pay toilets will be installed in federal buildings along with free toilets, and will also garner revenue for eliminating world hunger. Citizens will be given a choice as to how seriously they will take the term "comfort station."

I will encourage Americans to give up a meal each week and send the money saved to the federal government for foreign-aid food purchase. Restaurants will be asked to have containers to collect money which will be picked up periodically by postal agents. Supermarkets will have large containers into which shoppers can drop canned food and staple items to be sent overseas. The containers will be picked up periodically by Army trucks.

Children in elementary school will begin early to experience the joy and dignity of human service. I will initiate a Penny-a-Week Campaign in the public schools; a weekly collection deliberately low to avoid competition between rich and poor students. Nation-wide statistics for 1966 show an elementary and secondary school enrollment of 43,055,055. Average daily attendance was 39,366,000. The Penny-a-Week Campaign could collect almost $400,000 weekly to be used to extend world citizenship.

America must take leadership in eliminating world hunger. A nation in which poor folks on relief drink Diet-Rite can be satisfied with nothing less than providing a Right-Diet for the rest of the world.

CAUTION: CIGARETTE SMOKING MAY BE HAZARDOUS TO YOUR HEALTH

I can't understand people who keep on buying cigarettes. Now I don't mind catching cancer, but I'll be damned if I'm going to pay for it . . . and pay state and federal taxes. Of course, I stopped buying cigarettes when they put that little message on the pack: "Caution: Cigarette Smoking May Be Hazardous to Your Health." I'll be darned if I'm going to pay fifty cents a pack for some bad news . . . But really they ought to take that same message and stamp it on the side of our nuclear bombs. Of course, now that it's definitely proved that cigarettes cause cancer, I think they should go all the way and clean up those television commercials. I can just see it now. A cat would appear on the screen, light up a cigarette, take a deep draw and say, "Smoke cancer, kids" . . . Or a cat would appear with a big black ring around his tee-shirt and say, "I'd rather catch cancer than quit."

But Marlboro could have the most honest of the honest cigarette commercials. Have you ever seen that old Texan in the Marlboro ad? . . . Sitting on the fence in the big ten-gallon hat? . . . Barbecue sauce all over his face! . . . You *know* who that is! . . . Well, I'd take that same Texan and put him in front of a cemetery gate and have him slap his leg and say, "This is Marlboro country."

And I understand that Raleigh cigarettes are not going to have coupons on the back of the pack anymore. They've replaced them with Blue Cross-Blue Shield credit cards.

But I heard an old man on television the other day, who said he had been smoking for thirty years and has no intention of quitting. And I thought that was the most touching speech I had ever heard . . . from a guy in an iron lung.

Chapter VIII

CRISIS IN TOWN AND COUNTRY

The most critical national problem, affecting both town and country, is a shocking imbalance between population and land distribution in the United States. America is known as a land of plenty and, indeed, there is plenty of land; nearly 2.3 billion acres. Approximately 200 million Americans inhabit that land, about 140 million being jammed into the nation's cities. This means that 70 percent of the United States population occupies slightly more than 1 percent of the land! *SA*

Overcrowding on such a grand scale is unnatural and immoral. Since overpopulation is an unnatural phenomenon, overdeveloped land must inevitably manifest open denials of nature—crime, disease, ignorance and human misery. The conditions which prevail in our nation's cities are simply the result of too many people trying to live on too little land. Yet there are vast undeveloped areas in our nation. Underdeveloped and unspoiled land is natural and represents nature's bank account waiting to be developed and cultivated.

Over the past few decades, millions of Americans have left the country and headed into town. The lure of the city, with its employment opportunities, cultural advantages and so on, has been a magnetizing force to depopulate the countryside and overpopulate the metropolis. American cities have paid a heavy price for their popularity.

I have always maintained that New York City would

have a black majority if it hadn't been for the Negro pullman porters. As it stands today, Newark, New Jersey, has the majority and quite by accident. Most Negroes who came North were headed for New York. But when that train pulled into the next-to-the-last stop, and that porter came through yelling "Noo-aark," all the black folks got off a stop too early!

At least three-fourths of this nation's black population inhabit the major cities. Their rate of unemployment is double that of whites. Yet urban unemployment is not restricted to the black population. There simply are too many people in our major urban areas to provide jobs for everyone. The problem of unemployment cannot be solved until the prior problem of population redistribution is faced honestly and openly.

Creating a Work Force

I believe the federal government should take the initiative in encouraging a voluntary population redistribution. The federal government must take positive and determined creative action to *discourage* the population influx into the urban areas of this nation and to *entice* current urban dwellers to move into other areas. I propose the federal construction of industrial complexes. Like the Foreign Aid Factories, the industrial complexes would provide a work market for the unemployed in underdeveloped areas of the nation. In addition, they would make possible employment for those unemployed urban dwellers who would choose to move out of the city.

The federal government would simply build a standard building which could be appropriated by many different kinds of industry. The best architectural minds of the world should be encouraged to submit building plans. After a complex is completed, the federal government would abandon the project and encourage private industry to take over. Suppose, for example, Sears Roebuck chose to avail itself of such a free building and move into a particular area. Sears would be allowed to bring in 10 percent of the work force, that is, vocational trainers and other skilled personnel necessary to stimulate a local work force. Stress would be laid upon providing work for local unemployed of an underdeveloped rural area—those persons most receptive to the lure of the cities.

In addition, unemployed persons in the nation's cities would be encouraged to move to the industrial complex area to join the newly developing work force. To provide additional encouragement for such voluntary relocation, federal housing complexes would be built adjacent to the new industry. They would be model communities, fully equipped with health services, schools and recreational facilities. Day care centers would provide child care services for working mothers and employment for local people as baby sitters. Life in such model communities would be so imaginative and attractive, so creatively designed and planned, so enviably human, that the urban areas of the nation would suddenly lose their lure.

All public housing, whether located in town or country, should emphasize imagination and creativity. Public money spent for city housing projects should be invested in a new dimension of urban design and should give American taxpayers a sense of pride in having financed the latest innovations in architectural advance. The government should again solicit the consultation of the best architectural minds and enlist the advice of the world's leading experts in the area of developing human environment.

Residents of public housing projects should have a special pride in living in such an experimental community. Housing projects would become just what the name implies—projects to develop new ideas of living and use of space. Housing projects should be so exciting and beautiful that people will travel from other parts of the city just to look at them. All residents of a city should want to have a friend living in the projects so they could pay a visit. A beautiful new experience of human community would develop. Poor project dwellers would no longer be poor in spirit; they would be rich in pride and dignity. Yet one has only to look at the present eyesores which are the politicians' answer to public housing needs to see how far short of the vision the average city has fallen.

Toward a Better Environment

There are less imaginative, yet critically important measures which would create a more livable environment in both town and country. A federal law should be enacted prohibiting the cutting off of gas or heat during the winter months. And landlords whose buildings are without utilities during those months should be subject to severe prosecution. No heat and hot water during the freezing winter months is a great cause of hostility, bitterness and resentment in slum neighborhoods. It is the kind of thing which encourages oppressed people to riot. This is especially true when the poor have no other way to express their outrage. Every ghetto and slum neighborhood should have a 24-hour complaint department—a functioning department where complaints will be acted upon *immediately*.

A suggestion box should be attached to every mailbox in every city in the country. Citizens should know that they can drop their suggestions for improving life conditions in the corner mailbox. Rural residents can leave their suggestions in their own roadside mailbox. And every citizen should have the assurance that his suggestion will be read and considered. Private industry employs such a practice and often saves hundreds of thousands of dollars by implementing employee suggestions. The federal government just might save millions of dollars in property destruction by listening to the voice of the people.

Rebates should be given to residents of public housing projects who make a special effort to keep their apartments in good repair. Public housing residents must have some incentive to take good care of the space they occupy. For many Americans the incentive is property ownership. A reasonable rent rebate is no substitute for ownership. But it is a tangible expression which would encourage housing project residents to take pride in the space they call home.

Tax rebates should be used as incentives to fair employment practices. Any individual who works for a business or industry which definitely is an equal opportunity employer should get a 1-percent rebate on his income tax. Likewise, fair employment businesses and industries should get an equivalent tax break. I will propose such legislation as my administration's way of saying "thanks" to those in the private sector who believe and practice the values of dignity and freedom.

To begin immediately to create community in the midst of contemporary urban chaos, I will propose the formation of Neighborhood Unions. Such Unions will represent a return to a former concept of locality, which was the basis for government in this country until machine-dominated party politics took over. Community organization and citizen participation are so important that the federal government should assure their existence. Union representatives elected by residents of each neighborhood will be the advocates of the real needs of local communities. Such vital matters as public education policy or urban renewal plans could not simply be handed down from above but would become matters of collective bargaining between city government and Neighborhood Unions. Before urban renewal plans, for example, could be enacted, Neighborhood Unions would protect the rights of local residents. They would assure that the people who are being moved out of a renewal area would be the first new residents to move back in after completion of the renewal project. Though it is un-heard-of in our form of democracy, Neighborhood Unions would actually allow the *people* to tell the *government* what it can and cannot do.

The current poverty program is one of the most flagrant examples of the lack of citizen voice and the need for Neighborhood Unions. The big trouble with the poverty program is that the poor have not been able to get their hands on it. It remains the special possession of high-salaried administrators whose urban expertise is directly related to their friendship with politicians.

The poverty program must be taken from the politicians and given to the poor. Administration of the poverty program should be placed in the hands of the universities and the business community. When America needed a fast train, she gave the project to private industry and said: "Develop a high-speed train." Private industry did the research, developed the plan and put a fast train on the tracks between Boston and Washington. If the *politicians* in every regional area had been allowed to develop their own fast train, the money would have run out before the tracks were laid.

I would urge private industry and universities to develop projects which would meet the problems of depressed urban and rural areas and submit their proposals for government approval. Poverty money would be granted to the most rational and logical proposals. Industries working on poverty program projects would be given a certain amount of tax relief. Universities would be given research grants. For the first time the poverty program would be in the hands of those whose expertise is based on technical skill and knowledge. Representatives of poor communities receiving poverty program assistance would work in close consultation with the experts, and the technicians would be required to have all projects approved by the people themselves. In times of war, the private business sector and the government work hand in hand through government contract. The same should be true of the War on Poverty.

Starvation at Home

The crisis in town, country, government, indeed in all of American life, was revealed in its most tragic proportions in June, 1967. A report to the Field Foundation by a team of physicians investigating life in rural Mississippi said of the children there: "Not only are these children receiving no food from the government, they are also getting no medical attention whatsoever. They are out of sight and ignored. They are living under such primitive conditions that we found it hard to believe we were examining American children of the twentieth century."

The raw suffering of Mississippi children defies description. The doctors reported that almost every child they saw was in a state of negative nitrogen balance; which means that a marked inadequacy of diet has led the body to consume its own protein tissue. Children are doomed from the moment of conception because of the poor health of a mother and the absence of medical care. Again and again, the Field Foundation report documented that children are born injured, deformed or retarded because their mothers could not obtain the doctor or the hospital care they needed.

A glance at the 1968 Federal Budget indicates that, while the children were starving in Mississippi and other depressed areas of this country, North and South, the United States Information Agency was spending $191,-126,000; land and water conservation was costing the American taxpayers $3.5 billion; and $1,772 million was being sent overseas in the Food for Freedom program (which does not include foreign aid to develop food resources).

Official governmental response to hunger and starva-

tion in Mississippi was a food stamp program adminis-
tered by the Department of Welfare in Mississippi.
Under the program, money normally spent on food
could be redeemed for food stamps, $6 purchasing $10
worth of stamps. The stamps could be redeemed for food
at specified stores. But lethargy, ineptness, bureaucratic
entanglement and open racial discrimination combined
to make the food stamp program meaningless to the most
needy families of Mississippi. The Field Foundation report recommended: "The government should change its
system of welfare support, so that its funds directly reach
those who need them, without political or racial bias, and
reach them in an amount adequate to their minimum
needs for food, clothing, and medical care."

The supreme irony of American life is that governmental programs, supposedly designed to solve problems, in turn create them. The existence of a food stamp
program in Mississippi serves as a set of blinders for
governmental agencies, obstructing their vision of real
emergency situations. There is simply no reason at all
why food cannot be sent into such an emergency situation and distributed by the people themselves. The
Department of Agriculture has been empowered for such
action in emergency situations for more than thirty years.
Why must it take a tornado, a hurricane or a major fire
to force the admission of a state of emergency?

The current farm crisis, again the result of unwise and
insensitive governmental action, may create a nation-
wide famine which will make the Field Foundation report look like previews of coming attractions. Government control of crops and the rapidly disappearing small
farm have created a dangerous situation which could
affect the American food supply at any time.

American farmers no longer run their own farms or
plant what they feel they should. They follow the dictates
of government and its farm program. A farmer will not
risk being fined if he overplants. Food production in the

United States was once based on the law of averages. Thousands of operating farms throughout the country produced fine supplies of crops according to their own decision. When unseasonable weather hit one or more states, or even a group of states, the food production of thousands of other farms offset the unexpected losses.

This is not the case today. The trend of the diminishing small farm being replaced by large corporation-managed farms has already been noted. This trend began a few years ago after the government intervened in the personal operations of farms and made it impossible for a great number to operate at a profit. Rising food prices, feed, seed and labor shortages all contribute to the increased cost of operating a producing farm.

There is growing indication that America's food commitments will exceed her supply. The needs of the American bread basket, foreign aid commitments and the war effort could create a crisis of supply which could not be met by a decreasing number of farms producing under the standards of government control of crops.

A lesson from history should be heeded by the United States. Russia's attempt to control food and grain growth resulted in a food shortage. A solution was reached only when the decision was made to restore to the farmers greater freedom to run their own lives and to produce their own crops, without intervention and control by the government.

If famine strikes this country, and I fear that it may, the politicians will be responsible as they have been responsible for riots. After I am elected President, if there is still time, I will establish a National Advisory Commission on Rural Disorders to investigate thoroughly the farm situation and America's food supply. I personally think that this is an emergency. It would be ironic indeed if America discovered in the near future that our number one problem is not the racial problem but our food supply. My commission will have substantial representation from the farmers themselves and it will function to give farmers more say about growing the food which supplies the world.

About 80 percent of the land area of America can be used for agriculture. America *is* a land of plenty. But she is also a land of governmental mismanagement and political insanity. There is a simple governmental formula for *releasing* America's prosperity, both natural and human resources, rather than thwarting it, and it has been around now for some time: "Government of the people, by the people and for the people."

Can you believe we spent $30 million to take those crummy moon pictures . . . which were groovy pictures if you happen to dig holes . . . Now I don't want to knock progress, or anything, but I don't believe they went to the moon. I believe the space agncy got together and split that $30 million and took a closeup shot of some cold oatmeal . . . I showed those pictures to my daughter and she poured sugar and cream on them and tried to eat it.

And then how about those pictures we got back from Mars which were worse . . . They looked like the same pictures to me . . . Of course, everybody was disappointed, because they were looking for those itty-bitty green folks . . . What makes everybody think there's green folks on Mars? . . . Like they ain't ripe yet . . . Actually those pictures we got just might be them. They just might be one big swingin' bowl of oatmeal.

Trying to interpret those pictures makes about as much sense as some cats from Mars coming down and think they're taking pictures of us. Only what they didn't know is that they were taking pictures over a superhighway. And what they thought was us, was actually automobiles . . . I can see a group of top Martian scientists trying to interpret those pictures . . . "Yeah, they've got real intelligent life down there. They travel about eighty or ninety miles an hour . . . And they're real affectionate folks. They just keep bumpin' into one another . . . And at nighttime their eyes light up . . . And they have the strangest way of havin' sex. They pull into a little space and something strange comes out and sticks something into the rear . . . And you hear them say, 'Fill her up' . . . and you hear bells ring: 'Ding-ding-ding' . . . And sometimes they get real excited and say: 'Put a tiger in it.' "

Chapter IX

THE GREGORIAN COURT CALENDAR

The Constitution of the United States gives an American citizen the right to carry a gun to protect his life and property. Article II of the Bill of Rights states: "A well-regulated militia being necessary to the security of a free State, the right of the people to keep and bear arms shall not be infringed." I have profound respect for the Constitution and I think Article II of the Bill of Rights preserves an important right of every citizen. Yet passage of time and current events demand a reinterpretation of the original spirit and intent of that Article.

We must remember that there were no automatic weapons or no hand guns when the first ten amendments to the Constitution were written. Constitutional mandate was limited to shotguns and rifles. It is very difficult to slip a shotgun or a rifle into your pocket and travel across town. Anytime a man comes out of his home bearing a shotgun or a rifle, there is a good chance it will be noticed.

Even though I am nonviolent, I uphold the essential wisdom of the Constitution; namely, the right of a citizen to protect himself. The spirit of the Constitution guarantees the right of self-defense. And I happen to feel that a man can protect both himself and his family, or property, quite well with a shotgun or a rifle. I would urge gun legislation to interpret constitutional mandate to apply only to shotguns or rifles and to rule out small automatic weapons. The intent of the Constitution is to preserve a safe America. I feel this country is much safer in dealing with a man whose weapon can be seen than in dealing with a man who has a pistol hidden in his pocket.

I would also urge strict registration requirements for those who purchase guns. Fire arms were used to commit more than 6,500 murders and 43,500 aggravated assaults in 1966. If a man has to get a prescription to purchase medicine to cure disease, a man should also have to get some type of prescription to purchase a gun, which can do bodily harm to the well. A rigid reinterpretation of constitutional mandate regarding what type of weapon is legal and a strict registration requirement for legal weapons should be combined with stiff penalties imposed upon both the seller and the manufacturer of illegal weapons. Federal laws affecting the manufacturers and sellers of guns *must* be as rigid as federal laws *should* be against narcotics dealers and dope pushers.

It is the dope *pusher* who is the criminal and the dope *user* who is the sick man. Yet more poor, unfortunate, sick junkies find themselves prosecuted under current legal structures than pushers. Justice and humanity should demand treatment for the dope user's sickness and prosecution for the dope dealer's criminality. Putting the narcotics dealer out of business is a first step to treating the dope user's problem.

It is the same with gun manufacturers and gun sellers. Fear of prosecution at the source of the gun market would be a great deterrent to guns getting into the hands of potential criminals and would lessen the possibility of innocent victims being shot. The victims of gunshot wounds illegally inflicted, or their families, should be able, under federal law, to bring suit against the manufacturer and the seller of the gun.

Concern for the Cop

One of the most important issues in creating safe city streets is dealing fairly and justly with those who have the job of stopping crime in the streets; namely the cops. The cop has the most important and demanding job in the country and yet he is the most underpaid man in America. Society's unjust disregard for the cop is illustrated by the fact that the median annual pay for a cop in the large city is $5,300. Yet every time a riot breaks out in the ghetto, white America expects the cop to stop a problem he did not start.

I will propose federal legislation requiring the starting salary for cops in large cities to be a minimum of $10,-000 per year. Such legislation would go a long way toward establishing a new image for the cop. He will be more dedicated to his job, because he will be paid in proportion to the responsibility required of him. For the first time in America, the cop will have the dignity and respect he needs to begin to meet social problems rather than suppress them. Better qualified young men will be attracted to the career of law enforcement.

Under present conditions, it is impossible for the cop to perform his duties effectively. He is resented and distrusted in the ghetto because ghetto people have watched the cop's actions so carefully. They have seen the cop accept bribes from known criminals and look the other way when the pimp, the prostitute and the dope pusher conduct their business. The cop is abused by the politicians who expect him to clean up the mess the politicians themselves have made. Yet those same politicians do not respect the cop enough to pay him adequately.

Sending a cop into the ghetto to deal with social problems is like asking a sick doctor to operate on cancer. A doctor who has had cancer, tuberculosis, arthritis and polio might be very good at diagnosing symptoms because of past personal experience with disease, but I would not want him to operate on me while he is suffering an attack. Before society has a right to expect the cop to solve social problems, it must be willing to restore health to the police department.

While I feel the federal government should not intrude

into local police matters, there are certain measures which are the responsibility of federal government to initiate. I will propose a federal law that the family of any policeman killed in the line of duty will receive $10,-000. I will encourage scholarship funds for the orphan children of policemen killed in action.

I will further propose significant investment of federal funds in developing a unified nation-wide training program for policemen. Training centers will be established through federal government initiative. Veteran cops will be paid for their return to school. Training and retraining will emphasize developing skills in human relationships and understanding. The more knowledge the cop has, the less he will have to rely upon his night stick and his gun. For example, every ghetto uprising to date has been triggered by some action of a cop—an insensitive act which has blown off the lid of ghetto resentment. Once the rioting started, the cops could not stop it with their guns and night sticks. But if cops had been trained to be sensitive to ghetto needs and feelings, they would not have triggered the riot in the first place.

Every effort must be extended to overcome the breakdown in communication between the cop and the man in the street. Some people say taking away the cop's gun would be a first step in that direction. I propose instead to give all cops *two* guns. I would let the cops keep the revolver they now carry, but I would also require them to carry a tranquilizer gun. The cop would be expected to use the tranquilizer gun in every emergency which did not pose a definite threat to his own life. *Any* time a cop used his revolver, he would be subjected to thorough examination. I can see no excuse for a drunk or a kid being shot to death if a cop is carrying a tranquilizer gun. Ceasing the careless fire of the cop's revolver would go a long way toward establishing domestic tranquillity.

Programs must be designed to establish cooperative relationships between the police and the community.

Instead of urging ghetto dwellers to "Support Your Local Police," I would urge all police departments to "<u>Support Your Immediate Community</u>." Swimming pools, libraries and community centers should be built next to police precincts in ghetto neighborhoods. Kids would come to the precinct swimming pool to learn to swim and cops would serve as instructors and life guards. A new attitude toward the cop would automatically result. It is hard to hate a man wearing swimming trunks. Precinct libraries would give ghetto kids a place to do their homework in a quiet, warm, well lighted environment—a stark contrast to the crowded, rat-infested tenement apartments. Parents would know where their kids were at night. Strange new sounds would emanate from the ghetto. Parents would be heard saying, "Yes, Johnny's all right. He's over at the police station."

Cops would conduct classes at the community center for adults. Ghetto parents could come to the police station to learn first aid, artificial respiration, civil defense. Every effort would be made to create the working image of the police station as the vibrant center of community life rather than the cold symbol of community repression. People would come to the police station when their heat or light was off in their apartment and the police would be equipped to get immediate action. In such ways, a new era of police-community understanding could be opened up—all through a little enlightened initiative from the federal government.

The cop's image must be changed from that of an overseer of wrongs to an advocate of rights. Cops must spend time in the community talking to residents on a personal, nonofficial level. Cops must be seen to have a loyalty to the community in which they work. They must spend time informing community people of their rights under the law. Cops should sit down with people and carefully outline procedures of arrest and make sure they clearly understand what options are open to the man who is arrested. People do not associate the man in the blue uniform with a concern for their basic rights. Most people think of the lawyer when they think of their rights under the law. But if cops would spend time in the community making sure its residents thoroughly understand their rights under the law, they would acquire the same respect in the community as the lawyer. And this respect would be reflected in the community resident's attitude if and when he was arrested.

Police colleges should be established all over America which are as thoroughly and competent as FBI schools. A course in Police College should be from four to eight years. A massive recruiting effort should be made to encourage high school drop-outs to enroll in a Police College. Special emphasis should be made to enlist kids with police records. Police colleges should be highly technical, well equipped laboratories in crime prevention. Psychologists and sociologists should thoroughly school potential cops in the art of human understanding.

It is frightening to think that we send an astronaut into outer space and scientists on the ground know his heartbeat, his pulse rate and can read his brain waves, yet the cop on the corner does not know what is on the ghetto kid's mind. The best knowledge of modern science must be applied to the prevention of crime and the elimination of criminal motivation.

The elimination of criminal motivation must also be applied to the cop. The federal government should encourage the development of special service agencies for both cops and firemen. The cop and the fireman should have a place to go for help if he has a financial or family problem. The cop has too much responsibility to society to be on the street with a financial problem. He should never be tempted to accept a bribe or shake down a citizen.

During my administration, I will do everything in my power to bring justice to the policemen of America, because I will expect them to bring justice to the American people. As Peace President, I do not want a nation of cops. I do not want a police state. I am determined to create a well disciplined, well trained, humanely sensitive and thoroughly knowledgeable cadre of peace officers. And they will be paid in accordance with my high expectations of performance.

A Fireside Chat

The federal government must also take the initiative in developing modern techniques of fighting fires and assuring the use of the best possible equipment by the nation's firemen. Like the cop, the fireman is a vitally important member of the community. He can do much to build up community respect, inspire community confidence and promote community unity and well-being.

The crowded chaos of urban slums and ghettos is a massive firetrap. Every winter an alarmingly disproportionate number of black babies burn in urban fires due to the highly inflammable housing conditions in the black ghettos. Faulty heating and wiring contribute to make the ghetto a tinderbox. Each ghetto fire further inflames the resentment of its residents and the seeds of rioting are cultivated. Though firemen respond immediately to fire alarms, often the time spent in travel is the crucial time when lives are lost.

It is obvious you cannot take a fire to the fire station, but there is no reason you cannot bring the fire station to the fire. I propose roaming patrols of fire trucks in the slums and ghettos of the nation, keeping an all-night fire watch. Such fire patrols will be able to catch fires in the initial stages. Those crucial life saving moments for ghetto children will not be lost. Ghetto parents would be able to go to sleep at night during the winter months, closing their eyes comfortably for the first time. There is no doubt that a new feeling of trust, confidence and community would appear in ghetto neighborhoods.

I would encourage research in the use of helicopters for fire fighting. With the increase of automobiles jamming the urban streets, helicopters could be used to get firemen to a burning building more swiftly. Dropping firemen into a fire area from helicopters might be much safer than the use of ladders and would allow more direct access to a disaster area for the removal of trapped women and children. Perfection of the use of helicopters in fire fighting would have a pronounced effect on national security.

Imagine the effect upon the ghetto attitude if, after a winter of creative and imaginative fire fighting, every black ghetto resident knew a white fireman who had saved a black baby from burning to death. The prevention of babies burning might in turn prevent the cry of "Burn, baby, burn."

Kids in Trouble

The increase in crime among the youth of America is a serious symptom of national illness and unconcern. Arrests of juveniles for serious crimes increased 54 percent in 1966 over 1960. The number of persons arrested in the young age group, ten to seventeen years old, increased 19 percent. Auto theft increased 51 percent since 1960, and 80 percent of the offenders were young people under 25 years of age. Perhaps youth have been watching the actions of their elders a little too closely. It is worthy of mention that Senator Thomas Dodd chairs the Senate Subcommittee To Investigate Juvenile Delinquency in the United States.

Our society must engage in a thorough self-examination to determine the precise causes of delinquent behavior in youth. Every effort must be directed toward the prevention of delinquent youth becoming hardened criminals. Of the young offenders under twenty years of age released from a confinement in 1963, 65 percent were repeaters. America should thoroughly study life in societies which do not have a pronounced juvenile delinquency problem, comparing this nation to their standards to find out where we have gone wrong.

Television is a possible breeding ground for juvenile delinquency. The violence which invades every American living room each evening is not the best possible suggestion to an impressionable mind. It is the responsibility of the federal government to determine once and for all if television is a major contribution to the climate of crime. If so, television networks should be asked in no uncertain terms to clean up their programing. If they refuse, stiff federal penalties should be immediately forthcoming.

It is criminal negligence on the part of citizens at large to allow destructive influences to be attractively packaged for the consumption of youth. For example, it is definitely known that cigarettes are a major contributing factor to cancer. An America with the health of its young people at heart would insist that television cigarette commercials be outlawed.

The federal government should also sponsor studies of the correctional institutions confining juvenile offenders to see if they can be made into houses of *invention* rather than *detention*. Though it is unfortunate any time a young kid is jailed, the period of confinement should not be wasted. An institution which has complete control over a youth's allotment of time and privileges can control such things as study habits. Houses of correction should be converted into educational institutions and model experiences in group living. Such institutions should recognize and appreciate their unique opportunity to instill an appreciation of citizenship and responsibility in the most antisocial youth.

The nation should also take a good hard look at its court system. As President, I will make every effort to free the court system in America from political ties. I will seek federal legislation to rule out the concept of judgeship by political appointment. The court system should be operated with the same rational approach that defines a good hospital. Leading surgeons are not hired to top hospital positions because they are Democrats or Republicans, but rather because they are the best qualified men in their field. The judiciary system in America should follow that example. The judge determines the future of an arrested defendant much more than the cop.

The role of the judge should be raised to the highest possible moral plane. Favoritism and bias must be eliminated from the judge's bench. The deep-seated resentment among the ghetto poor is so often intensified in the court room. Ghetto people see the rich man given preferential treatment over the poor man. There is an old ghetto saying that "the rich man never gets the electric chair." Stiff penalties must be imposed upon those who would attempt to bribe a judge and upon the judges who accept such offers.

The federal government must take immediate action to insure legal representation for the poor. It is a sad day in America when the constitutional guarantee of any citizen depends upon the goodness of the American Civil Liberties Union's heart. America must find a way to make sure a poor man's case has as much chance of being heard by the Supreme Court as a rich man's case. I am sure that a government which is planning to land a man on the moon could solve the legal problems of the poor, if it were sincere. Yet it is easier today to land a man on the moon than to land a poor man's case in the Supreme Court.

I would propose federal subsidies to education for young men interested in becoming lawyers. The government would pay the way for such young men to attend law school. After graduation, the young lawyers would pay off their educational loan by spending a period of time handling the court cases of poor people. Another possible solution to the problem of the legally neglected poor would be a type of government controlled insurance program: a program for legal aid, like Blue Cross is for health services. Employers could take out legal insurance on their employees. Legal insurance would offset lawyers' fees as Blue Cross pays hospital expenses. There are many people in America today who would not receive hospital service apart from Blue Cross. America must find a way to extend this same principle to cover services in the courtroom.

After I am elected President, I will demand a thorough investigation of the use of the lie detector in America. The results of the investigation will be published, so that the American people will have a clear understanding of what the lie detector can and cannot do. Most people feel that the lie detector is infallible. Honest citizens ask for a lie detector test to prove their honesty. Through personal experience I have come to feel that the use of the lie detector is very close to a violation of constitutional rights.

In the early summer of 1965, I was arrested during the demonstrations in Chicago for school integration. I was accused of kicking and biting two cops. I knew I was innocent of the charge. The trouble was that I was also innocent of knowing the truth about lie detectors. I asked for and received a lie detector test. And, much to my surprise, I failed the test! It was a painful and embarrassing way to find out that lie detectors are not infallible and can be rigged against you.

If the investigation during my administration does not prove beyond the shadow of a doubt that lie detectors are absolutely trustworthy, I will urge federal legislation that they be outlawed and banned as a means of determining a man's guilt or innocence.

The concept of jury duty in America must be thoroughly re-evaluated. I believe current practice is outdated and outmoded. The cost of living in America is so high today that it is impossible to select a nonhostile jury. People should be encouraged to view jury duty as a privilege and an honor, rather than resenting being called, because they will miss a day's pay. The federal government should provide an incentive to accept jury duty, such as allowing a person to write a day's pay off his income tax for each day of jury duty served. The government should not only say to the American citizen that it is his duty to serve, but also that it is the government's duty to understand what service entails.

Federal legislation should be enacted which clearly states that *no* jury will be segregated. Trial by jury should assure a defendant that conviction will be because of guilt rather than color. I know of no other way to avoid the courtroom subtleties which produce lily-white juries than to state flatly in a federal law that juries will be integrated to reflect accurately the total population.

Article VIII of the Bill of Rights states: "Excessive bail shall not be required, nor excessive fines imposed, nor cruel and unusual punishments inflicted." Yet we still permit capital punishment in some states. I can think of no more *excessive* punishment than taking a man's life. Of course, though it is excessive, the taking of life is not *unusual* in this country. I vow to do everything in my power to abolish capital punishment after I am elected President. I personally feel that a Supreme Court decision is long overdue on Article VIII. I cannot see the "unusual'" practices of hanging, electrocuting, gassing or shooting another human being as anything other than a direct violation of the spirit of the Constitution.

Indeed America pays a high price for her cruel and unusual practice of killing. Ex-warden Jack Johnson of Cook County Jail in Chicago, one of the most outspoken critics of capital punishment, reports that it costs about $265,000 to kill a man who has killed. While this is only about half what it costs to kill a Vietcong, it is still a sizable figure. It only costs about $65,000 to incarcerate a man for life.

The average period of time between the death sentence and the actual execution is seven years. There are an unusual amount of legal expenses which become the burden of the state in capital offenses. The combination of a seven-year prison stay and the many legal fees produces the exorbitantly high price of state vengeance. America's image as a humane democratic nation is ridiculed the world over when it is realized that she will not only order and authorize the taking of life, but will also pay $265,000 for each thrill of vengeance.

As the New Year of 1966 began, there were 211,151 sentenced prisoners confined in state and federal institutions for adult felony offences in the United States. Supposedly, each of these prisoners was being rehabilitated.

Many of those fortunate enough to have been released over the past two years are unfortunately back behind bars. 67 percent of prisoners released early in 1963, after earning good time, were rearrested. There are ample statistics showing the return rate of persons who have served time to indicate that rehabilitation is not the dominant theme of prisons in this country. Prisons operate as places of punishment rather than rehabilitation.

A new emphasis upon rehabilitation must be instilled in all state and federal penitentiaries. From the first day the convicted man enters a penitentiary, he must be encouraged and enabled to submit his pattern of behavior to the expected norms of the world *outside*. The period of confinement should be a day-by-day preparation for the convict's return to the outside world. Too often prison life today is a day-by-day hustle to survive the strange world of confinement.

Prison jobs must reflect real job opportunities in the outside world. During their period of confinement, convicted men and women should receive vocational training and meaningful jobs. Decent recompense for actual work performed should be made to each prisoner, a substantial portion of which should be sent to the family back home. Thus the prisoner has a continued feeling of ongoing family support.

Every effort must be made to determine what made a prisoner go wrong—so that he can re-evalute his behavior pattern and make his second try at social adjustment successful. Prisoners should be allowed to wear civilian clothes on weekends. Certain prisoners, those who are not hardened criminals, should be allowed to leave the jail by day and continue in meaningful employment on the outside, returning to confinement in the evening. In such a manner a man could pay his debt to society without being prejudged a social outcast.

More sensitivity to the differences among prisoners should be displayed. Offenders of all ages, convicted of all types of crimes, should not be lumped together. Nineteen-year-old kids should never have contact with hardened criminals. Preoccupation with rehabilitation should always seek to find out what went wrong with a man's life rather than insisting that he be punished.

Each prison should have a free clothes center. When a man leaves confinement, he should do so with a decent wardrobe, not a cheap prison suit and $10 in his pocket. A thoroughly rehabilitated man needs attractive clothing for his new body and his new mind.

Rehabilitation concern should carry over into an ex-convict's new life in the outside world. If a man goes for five years without running afoul of the law again, he should come before a review board. If the board finds that he has indeed been living as a truly rehabilitated man, his former record should be sent to a private file in a federal location. It should never be made public again, for any purpose, unless the ex-convict is convicted again.

Rehabilitation means quite literally a second chance. It does not mean a partial chance with the stigma of a past mistake. Society can entice people to be good citizens by honestly being willing to forgive and forget. And rehabilitation can pay off. It reduces prison costs by decreasing the number of inmates. And the billions of dollars lost as a result of crime are recovered through rehabilitation.

The federal government should establish Crime Prevention Centers throughout the country—patterned after USO lounges. Such centers should be open twenty-four hours a day, attractively decorated, providing snacks and recreation. As soon as an ex-convict begins to get the feeling that he is drifting back into his former way of life, he should be able to go to a conveniently located Crime Prevention Center for guidance, counsel and acceptance. Crime Prevention Centers would provide an alternative for that poor man who feels compelled to throw a brick through a window because winter is coming on and he needs a place to stay. So he purposely commits a crime in order to get caught and escape the winter cold.

Some people will say that my suggestions are the visionary dreams of a utopian statesman, impractical, expensive and unrealistic. Such persons do not believe in humanity, nor in the real possibility of rehabilitation.

But I will continue to dream of a rehabilitated America.

THE CANDIDATE ON THE CANDIDATES

I understand LBJ has stopped watching television on Sunday afternoons. A few Sundays back Senator McCarthy was on *Face the Nation,* while Bobby Kennedy was on *Meet the Press.* On the other network they were showing *The Afternoon Movie,* starring Ronald Reagan!

I hope you all realize that Reagan spelled backwards is "nigger." That's why I hope Ronnie straightens himself out and goes on to become President of the United States. Just so we can say we got a backward nigger in the White House.

To be honest, Bobby Kennedy might not make such a bad President. If we were ever attacked by a foreign power, his family is large enough to defend, say, Rhode Island.

It looks like Richard Nixon might very well be the Republican nominee. I understand when Nixon was in college he was voted "Most Likely to Succeed—in coming in second."

If George Wallace wins the Presidential election, I'm going to take up a new profession. I'm going to become a foreign travel agent for Negroes.

Chapter X

PENCIL POWER

We have been on a visionary excursion together through the pages of this book. It was a short trip; but we've had time to share a few facts and figures, make some important observations and get terribly honest with one another. And I think we began to catch a glimpse of what life in America could be.

I like what I see when I let my imagination run wild. I like to think of the Constitution really working for everybody. I like to think of government money being creatively and honestly spent, free of graft, corruption and political manipulation. I see beautiful educational parks springing up in major cities all over this land. I see community people, who love their children, determining public educational policies. I see hospitals being constructed by the federal government in rural areas, witnessing to the people of the surrounding area that a man does not have to live in the city to be close to decent medical care.

I see the federal government encouraging young men and women to be doctors and nurses and financing their education. And I see those young graduates paying back five years of service in one of the newly constructed hospitals. I see an industrious, honest, low-income working man, with a hunger to expand his knowledge, coming home at the end of the day and switching on the 24-hour-a-day educational TV channel which has just been initiated by a government grant.

Dreams? Visions? Yes, of course. But, then, I have always been a dreamer, as were the Sons of Liberty and the framers of the Declaration of Independence. And I think secretly in the mind of every citizen there is the faint whisper of the American Dream. I am asking you to continue with me on my political trip; to join me in increasing that whisper to a resounding chorus. I am asking you to Write Me In!

I will not be conducting a slick, well financed campaign. My campaign will definitely be a shoestring operation. Black folks have been hearing white folks tell them to "pick themselves up by their own boot straps" for so long, that I know of no other way to operate. I will be speaking throughout the country for the next few months, telling the truth, expanding mental horizons and urging voters to be independent and exercise their right of pencil power.

Remember to bring your own pencil with you when you go to vote in November. If you are using a voting machine, you will notice a small door on the face of the machine, usually in the upper left-hand corner. The door slides up, exposing a square of blank paper. You simply write in the name "Dick Gregory."

If you are using a paper ballot, write the word "President" and draw a square box next to it on the right. Place an X in the box and print "Dick Gregory" next to the box on the right.

The above instructions are standard and will apply to most states. I urge you, however, to take the initiative in finding out rules governing the Write-In vote in your own state.

And when you are in Washington, D. C., next year, be sure to drop by my new House. Remember the name, "Dick Gregory." That's D-I-C-K G-R-E-G-O-R-Y.

To *see* how to
Write Me In,
turn page.